Surprised by
France

by
Donald Carroll

SURVIVAL BOOKS • LONDON • ENGLAND

First published 2005

Survival Books Limited
26 York Street, London W1U 6PZ, United Kingdom
☎ +44 (0)20-7788 7644, 🖷 +44 (0)870-762 3212
✉ info@survivalbooks.net
🖳 www.survivalbooks.net
To order books, please refer to page 239.

British Library Cataloguing in Publication Data.
A CIP record for this book is available
from the British Library.
ISBN 1 901130 44 4

Printed and bound in Italy by Legoprint spa.

Acknowledgements

I would like to thank Joe Laredo for the close attention and thought he put into editing this book, which is clearly the better for his wise interventions, Kerry Laredo for the stylish and unfussy format, and Jim Watson for his clever illustrations and eye-catching cover design. Most of all, I am indebted to all my friends and neighbours in France, who will never know how much they have helped because I intend to keep it a secret from them, and to my wife, who will tell them anyway.

DC

Titles by Survival Books

Alien's Guides
Britain; France

The Best Places To Buy A Home
France; Spain

Buying A Home
Abroad; Cyprus; Florida;
France; Greece; Ireland; Italy;
Portugal; South Africa; Spain;
Buying, Selling & Letting
Property (UK)

Foreigners Abroad: Triumphs & Disasters
France; Spain

Lifeline Regional Guides
Costa Blanca; Costa del Sol;
Dordogne/Lot; Normandy;
Poitou-Charentes

Living And Working
Abroad; America;
Australia; Britain; Canada;
The European Union;
The Far East; France; Germany;
The Gulf States & Saudi Arabia;
Holland, Belgium & Luxembourg;
Ireland; Italy; London;
New Zealand; Spain;
Switzerland

Making A Living
France; Spain

Other Titles
Renovating & Maintaining
Your French Home;
Retiring Abroad

Order forms are on page 239.

WHAT READERS & REVIEWERS HAVE SAID

If you need to find out how France works, this book is indispensable. Native French people probably have a less thorough understanding of how their country functions.

LIVING FRANCE

This book is a Godsend – a practical guide to all things French and the famous French administration – a book I am sure I will used time and time again during my stay in France.

READER

I would recommend this book to anyone considering the purchase of a French property – get it early so you do it right!

READER

Let's say it at once: David Hampshire's *Living and Working in France* is the best handbook ever produced for visitors and foreign residents in this country. It is Hampshire's meticulous detail which lifts his work way beyond the range of other books with similar titles. *Living and Working in France* is absolutely indispensable.

RIVIERA REPORTER

I found this a wonderful book crammed with facts and figures, with a straightforward approach to the problems and pitfalls you are likely to encounter. It is laced with humour and a thorough understanding of what's involved. Gets my vote!

READER

I was born in France and spent countless years there. I bought this book when I had to go back after a few years away, and this is far and away the best book on the subject. The amount of information covered is nothing short of incredible. I thought I knew enough about my native country. This book has proved me wrong. Don't go to France without it. Big mistake if you do. Absolutely priceless!

READER

If you're thinking about buying a property in France, Hampshire is totally on target. I read this book before going through the buying process and couldn't believe how perfectly his advice dovetailed with my actual experience.

READER

ABOUT OTHER SURVIVAL BOOKS ON FRANCE

In answer to the desert island question about the one how-to book on France, this book would be it.

THE RECORDER

It's just what I needed! Everything I wanted to know and even things I didn't know I wanted to know but was glad I discovered!

READER

There are now several books on this subject, but I've found that this book is definitely the best one. It's crammed with up-to-date information and seems to cover absolutely everything.

READER

Covers every conceivable question concerning everyday life – I know of no other book that could take the place of this one.

FRANCE IN PRINT

An excellent reference book for anyone thinking of taking the first steps towards buying a new or old property in France.

READER

Thankfully, with several very helpful pieces of information from this book, I am now the proud owner of a beautiful house in France. Thank God for David Hampshire!

READER

I saw this book advertised and thought I had better read it. It was definitely money well spent.

READER

We bought an apartment in Paris using this book as a daily reference. It helped us immensely, giving us confidence in many procedures from looking for a place initially to the closing, including great information on insurance and utilities. Definitely a great source!

READER

A comprehensive guide to all things French, written in a highly readable and amusing style, for anyone planning to live, work or retire in France.

THE TIMES

Editor's Notes

- This is neither a 'how to' book nor a guide book but is intended to provide an insight into – and in some cases an explanation of – certain peculiarities of the French way of life. All such observations are based on the experience of the author and may differ from those of other observers of French life and culture.

- A list of websites where further information on topics referred to in this book can be found is on page 228.

- French words and phrases are italicised and important words set in bold type.

- The following symbols are used in this book: ☎ (telephone), 📠 (fax), 🖳 (internet), ✉ (email).

The Author

Donald Carroll is known on both sides of the Atlantic for his humorous books as well as a number of travel guides, including the award-winning *Insider's Guide to Turkey*. Formerly a columnist and broadcaster, he has written for *The Observer, The Independent* and *Private Eye* and, on the other side of the Pond, for the *New York Times, Los Angeles Times, American Heritage* and *Playboy*. He has lived in France for nine years.

CONTENTS

SURPRISINGLY ENOUGH . . .

To hear most people tell it, the only surprising thing about France or the French is that there are any surprises left. After all, as the world's most popular tourist destination, France has more visitors in any given year than it has inhabitants. And of those inhabitants more than a million are British and at least 100,000 are Americans. Add to these migratory numbers our shared history: Britain and France have been next-door neighbours since time began, while the US and France have been best friends ever since the French crucially intervened on the Americans' side in their War of Independence. No wonder we think we know all there is to know – or all that really matters – about the French.

It was one of America's Founding Fathers and most ardent Francophiles, Thomas Jefferson, who perhaps best summed up this attitude. "France", he once famously said, "is every man's second country."

Yet it's precisely because we have so long presumed that we possess some special knowledge of France that Europe's largest country still remains a vast, uncleared minefield for English-speaking visitors and immigrants alike. We and the French go back far enough to have become part of each other's mythology. Casual misinformation has had time to congeal into rigid misconception, wild guesses have had time to become domesticated as hard facts, odd types have grown into stereotypes, anecdotes have become examples. Even those who consider themselves to be experts, for instance, on French etiquette seem to be unaware that the word *étiquette* itself rarely has the same meaning in French as it has in English.

Indeed it's the *soi-disant* experts themselves who have probably done most to perpetuate some of the more ludicrous myths about the French. In a way this is understandable. Without myth-making, how can one begin to explain that, although the French work only a 35-hour week, take a two-hour lunch, are never seen to exert themselves, and have chronically high unemployment, burdensome taxes and a suffocating bureaucracy, they still manage to enjoy manifest prosperity in the world's fifth largest economy? Or how do we reconcile the fact that the very people who eat the richest food, drink the most wine, and smoke far too many cigarettes are the same people who have the second-longest life expectancy in the world, after the Japanese? Why, for that matter, does the country with the stiffest driving test and the best roads produce the worst drivers? And how on earth can France's sublime art and architecture have survived, and thrived, alongside the world's most hideous wallpaper?

Of course, the easiest way to resolve these apparent discrepancies and contradictions is to construct overarching myths that can accommodate them. (Mrs Thatcher, as she then was, came up with the ultimate in one-size-fits-all explanations for Gallic behaviour when she said, understandingly, of President Mitterrand: "He's French, you know.") The usual process by which observable truths are converted into laughable untruths goes something like this: The French eat frogs' legs (true); so they must find frogs especially tasty (not true); that's why the French are called 'Frogs' (not true). Or: The French drink a lot of wine (true); as a result, they don't drink much water (not true). Or: The French never drink coffee during their meals (true); so they mustn't like coffee (not true).

It's out of little counterfeit syllogisms such as these that grow the myths which eventually shed their 'tips' and 'helpful hints' onto the unwary.

But at least this is all harmless nonsense. Where it starts to become damaging is when the advice takes the form of warnings based on an author's own unhappy experience. When one reads, for example, that the French are difficult to make friends with, that they will seldom if ever invite you to dinner, that they will despise you for not speaking French properly, that you can expect to be excluded from family occasions such as weddings, that you may well be bullied by the *gendarmes* and will almost certainly be treated with indifference or contempt by shop assistants, these aren't so much the sage words of a cosmopolitan traveller as the wounded cries of an international misfit. The problem is that, if taken seriously, they become self-fulfilling prophecies – which probably accounts in part for the fact that, of the estimated 50,000 Britons who move to France each year, well over half return home within two years.

That still leaves a lot behind, many of whom, sadly, live in the shadows of the same artificial gremlins that frightened off the others. In a parody of the natural tendency of expatriates to circle their wagons in unfamiliar territory, they tend to cluster in areas like the 'Dordoyne', where they spend their days in Bermuda shorts and sandals with socks – always with socks – playing bridge and watching cricket on satellite television, speaking nothing but English and discussing – endlessly discussing – property values over their gin-and-tonics. They can be easily recognised at a distance by their tribal call: "This is the life!"

For these people, it must be said, France holds few surprises, if only because they seldom wander off their reservations; when they do, it is as tourists on a short break. Nor are they surprised – startled perhaps, but not surprised – by the attitudes or behaviour of the natives because, well, they're French, you know.

Which brings me to the central dilemma facing anyone who would attempt to identify the surprises that new arrivals in France are likely to encounter: how does one decide what is surprising and what isn't? If I stuck to things that still surprise me after almost a decade living here, the result would be a fairly esoteric pamphlet. On the other hand, if I included everything I know of that has ever surprised somebody at some time, I would end up compiling a massive, and massively tedious, encyclopaedia of the obvious.

My first inclination is to err on the side of inclusiveness, on the grounds that it's preferable to risk repeating what may be common knowledge among the many than it is to risk withholding potentially helpful information from the few. But even that unobjectionable principle fails to take into account the possibility that what I assumed to be the few may well be in the majority. I made this worrying discovery while watching *The Weakest Link*, a television quiz programme that would more aptly be called *The Missing Link*, given the evolutionary back numbers among its contestants. From these benighted souls I learned that Berlioz and Ravel were Austrian, Sartre was Italian, Cézanne and Monet were stalwarts of the Renaissance, Louis XVI was married to Anne Boleyn, and Paris is the site of the Leaning Tower of Pisa. As if that weren't depressing enough, I then picked up a popular guidebook to France, where I learned that Americans are surprised by such 'unusual' foods as asparagus, rabbit and chicory.

So much for the inclusiveness principle. In the end, I decided to limit the book's scope to those occurrences and situations that any intelligent person new to France might reasonably find surprising – plus those things that everybody already knows, but that still haven't lost their power to surprise even longtime residents. French drivers, for example, who despite being infamous for their bad driving can still surprise you if you aren't constantly expecting a near-death experience. Similarly, although you're probably aware that the French have a relaxed, unembarrassed approach to bodily functions, you may not be totally prepared for unisex toilets, or for men casually urinating beside the road, or for the *grande dame* who responds to your polite enquiry about her health with an unforgettably detailed inventory of the contents of her toilet bowl. Ready or not, these things get your attention.

What I have deliberately excluded is any serious effort to unravel the mysteries of the French legal system, educational institutions, civil service, tax structure, economy, housing market, or tourist attractions, to name only a few of the complex areas where there already exists a huge specialist literature. For a proper study of these subjects the reader is referred to the last chapter, **The Safety Net**, in which I have listed websites of particular interest.

Finally, I should emphasise that the chapters aren't organised according to any known principle of taxonomy. The entries are where they are simply because there happened to be vacancies on my train of thought at the time. Consequently, the placing of many of the surprises I have chosen may well seem arbitrary, if not eccentric.

Or, to put it another way, surprising.

Donald Carroll
April 2005

1.

SOME SURPRISING THINGS ABOUT
FRENCH SOCIETY

There's an old saying in France that when describing the population of a city Americans will say theirs has 100,000 inhabitants, the British will say theirs has 100,000 souls, and the French will describe theirs as home to 100,000 French people.

Although the French are thought of as among the most exclusive and unwelcoming of nationalities, they are in fact much quicker than the British to bestow the advantages of citizenship on those caught up in the aftermath of their imperial adventures. In addition, France has a long and honourable tradition of providing a refuge for the victims of tyranny and persecution, irrespective of their political persuasion – unlike the UK and the US, who aren't known for sheltering foreigners with unfriendly opinions.

~~~~~

Once you're French, that's it.

You're never skewered on ethnic hyphens: Afro-French, Franco-Caribbean, Franco-Swiss, French-Canadian, etc. The only thing that matters is that you're French. Likewise, your religious or political beliefs have no bearing whatever on your Frenchness. It would be unthinkable for the French to pledge allegiance to a nation state 'under God', as the Americans do, or to regard working for the Communist Party as an 'un-French activity', or to consider a marriage valid that had only the blessing of a religious group.

~~~~~

French documents and questionnaires do not ask for information about your ethnic background.

The same goes for your religious affiliation and first language. Such intrusive questions are considered anathema in a republic that has banished considerations of blood, faith and language as criteria for citizenship. Consequently, reliable statistics are sometimes hard to come by.

~~~~~

The French don't distrust foreigners.

They distrust strangers. As a matter of fact, they tend to prefer foreigners to native strangers. Foreigners have an excuse for their unfamiliar behaviour, and are therefore granted a partial exemption from the lesser rules that govern French socialising. French people, lacking any such diplomatic immunity, have a harder time of it. And everyone hates Parisians.

~~~~~

French conversation isn't as argumentative as it appears.

The French consider small talk as at best a waste of time; at worst, it's a misuse of the language and an insult to the intelligence. A passionate, even heated, discussion of the merits of a particular wine is considered a much more interesting exercise than, say, gossip about the virtue of the *vigneron*'s wife.

~~~~~

The French are Europe's most dedicated rule-makers.

The French believe profoundly that everything that matters should be done in the right way at the right time. Ever since Napoleon drew up the *Code Civil*, it has been thought necessary to codify all aspects of public life. No regulation is too obscure, no protocol too outdated, to escape the attention of the state's official watchdogs. Whether it's the purity of French grammar or the pecking order of the bureaucracy, some things are simply inviolable. If you doubt this, see **Chapter 12**.

~~~~~

The French are Europe's most dedicated rule-breakers.

While the French feel it's their God-given duty to impose order and logic on the disorderly and illogical, at the same time they respect the contradictory right of the individual to override minor, annoying restrictions such as those that apply to when and where one can walk, drive, park, smoke, etc. And when it comes to sidestepping major infringements of one's personal freedom – such as the requirement to pay taxes – the French have an aptitude bordering on genius.

In fact, the array of techniques employed to outwit the bureaucrats has its own quasi-bureaucratic name: *Système D*. Loosely translated as 'resourcefulness', *Système D* derives from the reflexive verbs *se débrouiller* (to get by) and *se démerder* (literally, to get oneself out of the *merde*).

This unashamedly dual approach to the rule of law is nowhere better seen than in France's relationship with the European Union. While the French have devised most of the laws that govern the EU, they also have more court rulings against them for violations of EU law than any other member state. The European Commission has now threatened France with fines unless they begin taking notice of decisions by the European Court of Justice. The Commission successfully instituted proceedings against France six times between 2001 and 2004 – and the French government ignored all of them.

The French are snobs.

Where British snobbery is based on hereditary class distinctions and a long imperial memory, and American snobbery is based on unchallenged military might and the myth of the self-made man that they've confected out of a deprived sense of history, French snobbery is based on an innate sense of style, of what is in good taste and what isn't. This 'style' is almost impossible to pin down, but it gives the French what Walpole denounced as "their insolent and unfounded airs of superiority". In any case, however one defines the uniquely French sense of style, it's probably fair to say that the snobbishness it breeds is the least stylish thing about the French.

~~~~~

The French invented the subtlest power-dressing in the world.

Madame de Staël, Napoleon's nemesis, always held a small leafy twig, which she twirled constantly to draw attention to the fact that she had very beautiful hands. And in what other country would the head of state have a mother-of-pearl button sewn on to his suit jackets in order to catch the eye when he appeared in group photographs with other world leaders?

~~~~~

Tourism has created a new growth industry.

Thanks to the boom in tourism, certain types of crime are booming as well in France. There was always an epidemic of pickpockets in Paris; now it's a plague. And household burglaries are soaring to keep pace with the rapidly increasing number of holiday homes and gîtes. But the most startling increase has been in the number of car thefts, especially in the South of France, where thieves target vehicles with registration numbers from other parts of France or Europe.

~~~~~

The French like their home-grown businesses to be run from home.

Only three of France's 50 largest firms are run by foreigners. In Britain the figure is 17.

~~~~~

The French like to admire Americans from afar.

Although the French have long been enchanted by such quintessentially American inventions as the Bill of Rights, the cowboy, and jazz, they're the only group in Europe that has never at some point emigrated *en masse* to America.

~~~~~

The family comes first.

In France the family far outranks everything else in importance. While marriage is a desirable preliminary to taking on the responsibilities of an adult, it's having children that marks the onset of real adulthood. That's where the serious obligations and lifelong commitments begin. Everything else comes second to being a parent. Above and beyond the basic parental responsibility for the protection, care and feeding of one's offspring, there's in France the added duty to civilise them.

Nor do the family obligations end there. Just as parents are expected to look after their young, so children are expected to look after their parents in old age. Indeed, France is one of the few countries that has not only a highly developed foster care programme for children but also a parallel programme for fostering the elderly in family homes. In the killer heat wave of 2003, what shocked the French was not the number of elderly who perished but the number of bodies that remained unclaimed. Where were their families?

~~~~~

The Frenchman of the beret and the accordion is an endangered species.

In fact, he's on the verge of extinction. There are only three manufacturers of berets left in France, all of them in the south-west near the town of Pau, and they've survived only because they diversified into other headgear. Together they produce no more than a million berets a year, a third of which go to the French army. The future for the accordion, France's long-beloved 'piano of the poor', looks similarly bleak. Its principal factory, in Tulle, which turned out 6,000 accordions annually before the Second World War, now produces just 800 a year.

~~~~~

The French judge themselves according to different criteria than other people.

In a survey of 30 countries, people were asked which was more important: who they were or what they had achieved. Most said that what they had achieved was more important, with the US and the UK heading the list. The French were top of those who ranked above all else who they were.

~~~~~

The French take a uniquely aesthetic approach to otherwise 'functional' public projects.

The latest and most breathtaking example is the beautiful Millau viaduct, the world's highest bridge, in the Aveyron. Not only does it bring the Mediterranean hours closer to travellers from the north, but it's gently curved so that motorists using it can also appreciate its beauty.

~~~~~

Friendship is a serious matter in France.

As often as not, friends in English-speaking countries are little more than upgraded business associates, golfing partners, classmates, or names on one's Christmas card list. In France, by contrast, friends are those select few who have earned your trust, respect, and loyalty. You're committed to each other, and you participate in each other's lives. A friend is here today, and here tomorrow. It's impossible to explain this to anyone who regards friends as collectibles, or witnesses to one's likeability.

A now-famous experiment was conducted some years ago in which large numbers of various nationalities were set the following problem: You are the passenger in a car driven by a friend. The driver is doing 35mph in a zone where the speed limit is 20. The car hits a pedestrian. There are no witnesses. The driver stops to help the injured pedestrian, and reports the accident, but claims to have been driving under the speed limit. You're advised by your friend's lawyer that if you corroborate this version of events you will save your friend from the consequences of speeding. What do you do?

Only 5 per cent of the Americans, and 10 per cent of the British, said they would lie to protect their friend. But 32 per cent of the French said they would be willing to bend the truth if it would help a friend.

While the results refer to a specific set of circumstances, and so can hardly be used to prove a wider point, they do suggest that a gulf exists between the Anglo-American and the French ideas of friendship.

~~~~~

The bourgeoisie isn't a class.

It's three classes, actually. The *grande bougeoisie* are what the name implies: grand, sometimes very grand. The grandest of the families in this class tend to carry a *de*, as in de Gaulle, and are often descended from the pre-Revolutionary nobility. The *bonne bourgeoisie* are the Establishment-in-waiting, the ones on the way up, the ones who will be responsible for making the country work. The *petite bourgeoisie* are the closest equivalents the French have to our lower middle class: the objects of everyone else's contempt, desperate not to appear working class but doomed to be kept in their place by those above them on the social ladder.

~~~~~

No wonder Paris is called the City of Light.

The Paris *hôtel de ville* (city hall) has 1,290 windows and 142 Baccarat crystal chandeliers.

The city's open spaces include 6,425 acres of parks and gardens, tended by 4,200 gardeners.

~~~~~

Until recently, French parents could give their children only state-approved names.

This isn't as outrageous as it may sound, or as restrictive. I've often thought that one of the worst forms of child abuse was the burdening of one's children with ludicrous names that mark them for life as surely as any stigmata. Whether the result of capriciousness or thoughtlessness – or, worse, a willingness to use the child as a billboard for a political statement – the bestowing of a ridiculous name has only one effect: to label the child as someone whose own parents were prepared to forfeit his or her right to be treated with simple dignity. And given that the entire machinery of French law is geared towards the inclusion and acceptance of individuals as citizens with equal rights, it does seem illogical to allow some people to undermine this ideal by branding their children in order to proclaim their separateness.

In any case, the law has now been abandoned, so that we're already seeing in the desolate *banlieues* that fringe the larger French cities the same phenomenon that characterises British and American urban slums: an underclass instantly identifiable by names that could have been spooned out of a bowl of alphabet soup. Thus do the underprivileged find new ways of depriving themselves.

And now French lawmakers have found a new way to vex genealogists: by making it permissible to use the paternal, maiden or both family names for newborn children there.

The middle classes, meanwhile, are currently demonstrating a taste for English names. In the 'Births' column of the local newspaper in front of me, I see the following sprinkled among the more classic French names: Jemima, Rosa, Catherine, Laura, Audrey, Laetitia, Nelly, Sarah, Damien, Robin, Arthur, Mark and, believe it or not, Marilou.

~~~~~

The French often prefer artificial flowers to real ones.

At least, they often prefer buying the artificial kind, which jostle for space with real ones in florists' shops. The only plausible explanation for this lapse in taste is the presence of a mutant gene in the French population that also makes itself known in the form of that ugly floral wallpaper one often finds on French walls – and doors, and ceilings . . .

~~~~~

The French like to refer to their country as the Hexagon.

Some commentators have adduced this as evidence that the French are inward-looking, insular. This may well be the case, but I must say I fail to see the connection. If anything, French history would suggest they're outward-looking, sometimes to an overbearing extent, while geography (and literalism) would suggest they're peninsular rather than insular.

Nor does it take much imagination to see that France is roughly hexagonal in shape, its six sides being formed by the English Channel and the Atlantic to the west, the Pyrenees and the Mediterranean to the south, with the Alps and the Rhine marking the eastern flank, up to the point where the northern border wiggles westward from Alsace through the Ardennes back to the Channel above Dunkirk. Thus, far from indicating a need to enclose France within artificial boundaries, the idea of France as a hexagon would appear to be the result of a typically French effort to introduce the order of geometry to the unpredictable disorder of the land – in other words, to straighten Nature's lines a little.

2.

SOME SURPRISING THINGS ABOUT
FRENCH CULTURE

All countries value their cultural heritage in their own way and with varying degrees of pride. Nobody, however, can match the French for their devotion not only to their own resplendent culture, but also to the idea of culture itself.

In France, culture isn't something that other people have. It's as essential to life as sunlight.

Whereas in most countries there's a 'cultured' elite that act as guardians of the artistic and intellectual patrimony of the nation, in France there's something more akin to a people's militia. That's no exaggeration. When Cézanne complained to his local Prefect of Police that he couldn't work for the barking of the dogs in his neighbourhood, the order was immediately given to lock up all the local dogs while the great man was painting.

Nor is such deference reserved for the great and the gifted. To take just one example, chosen specially for its persuasiveness: Shortly after moving to France, I was stopped by a *gendarme* for driving too fast, way too fast, through a town. As he wrote out the ticket, the gendarme explained that for such an offence I was liable for an on-the-spot fine. I didn't need to be told that the fine would be heavy. He then asked what I did for a living. I said I was a writer. "Oh," he said, as if he had just remembered something important. Deciding to push my luck, I added: "A poet." The upshot was that the ticket was suddenly in shreds, and I was being asked for the titles of any of my books that were available in French, before being waved on my way with what amounted to an apology for keeping me from doing the Lord's work.

I like to fantasise about some day telling a highway patrolman in, say, Alabama that I was hurrying home to finish a sonnet.

Literary ability is a significant aid to a political career.

Lamartine, de Tocqueville and Chateaubriand were all distinguished 19th-century men of letters who rose to become Foreign Ministers. More recently, President Giscard d'Estaing was an acknowledged expert on Maupassant, while his Prime Minister, Raymond Barre, was an expert on Baudelaire. President Mitterrand was himself the author of nine books, and President Chirac has publicly declared that "poetry is a necessity of daily living". (His favourite poets are the rather oddly coupled Verlaine and Apollinaire.)

To get a good idea of how this association with literature plays with the electorate, one has only to recall the famous occasion when Giscard took time off in the midst of a political crisis to appear on a television programme about the work of Maupassant. Not only did Giscard's standing in the polls shoot up, so did sales of Maupassant's books.

~~~~~

France's love affair with her intellectuals is genuine.

When the American writer and critic Susan Sontag died at the end of 2004, the obituarist for *The Economist* wrote: "It's hard to be an intellectual in the United States. In France, a wizened man or woman in a black beret, smoking unfiltered Gitanes and with a copy of Sartre's *La Nausée* in his pocket, is considered a national treasure."

It's perhaps worth remarking here that when Sartre died in 1974, 600,000 people followed his funeral procession.

The world's largest library and largest museum are both in Paris.

They are the Bibliothèque Nationale and the Louvre.

Some of the world's worst libraries are also in France. Outside the main cities, it's amazingly rare to find really good public libraries.

~~~~~

French intellectuals nonetheless feel insufficiently loved by their government.

Recently 40,000 intellectuals signed a petition accusing the French government of waging a 'war on intelligence'. They complained that French education had become little more than vocational training, while French culture was becoming a branch of the entertainment industry. As a result, they argued, knowledge was now simply a means to an end rather than an end in itself, and therefore intellectuals were increasingly being sidelined as irrelevant. In reply, the education minister dismissed their complaints with the unhelpful observation that intellectuals were "not a protected species".

~~~~~

Popular music isn't one of the glories of French culture.

One is tempted to go further and say that for some reason music has never been among the things that immediately come to mind when considering France's gifts to the world. In view of this, it's perhaps cruel to narrow the focus to contemporary pop music, which in France has long been dominated by the vocally-challenged and surgically re-surfaced mediocrity, Johnny Hallyday.

No one, to my knowledge, has ever satisfactorily explained the Hallyday phenomenon. Almost anywhere else he would be a national joke. Yet in France he is, in the words of a recent magazine article, "an institution, a national monument and, above all, a living legend". The numbers are there to prove it: he has sold hundreds of millions of records, starred in 28 films, and is the subject of 30 internet websites. God knows why. The only plausible theory I've been able to come up with is that the French, unable or unwilling to compete on the vulgar level of most contemporary music, deliberately invented a joke singer with a joke name to see how long it would take the rest of us to cotton on. However, when I put this theory to a usually sophisticated French lady of my acquaintance, I was swiftly and brutally persuaded of the error of my thinking. I give up.

~~~~~

Reading is popular in France. So is not reading.

The good news is that 18 per cent of French adults claim to read 25 or more books a year. The bad news is that roughly the same number either don't or cannot read at all. (The majority of those in between say they read at least ten books a year.)

Their newspaper-reading habits are more American than British, in that they tend to read local or regional papers instead of national ones. France's biggest-selling daily, somewhat improbably, is *France-Ouest*, published in Rennes. As for magazines, the French are omnivorous; accordingly, France produces more magazines than any other European country.

Strangely for a country with such a large anglophone population, until recently France didn't have a single decent homegrown newspaper in English. But in March 2005 the Parisian daily *France Soir* began publishing a weekly edition in English, which should help fill this gap.

~~~~~

Columbo is more popular in France than Poirot.

He's so popular, in fact, that *un lieutenant Columbo* has entered the language as the prototype dogged investigator, while Peter Falk has been made a *Chevalier des Arts et Lettres*. Not that Monsieur Poirot doesn't have his loyal following – but he **is** Belgian, you know.

~~~~~

You can trust everything you read in Le Monde except the date.

France's most respected national newspaper is both thoughtful and accurate, but it does allow itself one small liberty: it plays fast and loose with the calendar. When it hits the streets in Paris in the afternoon it carries the following day's date, because subscribers outside Paris receive their copies by post the next morning and presumably don't like the idea of reading yesterday's newspaper.

~~~~~

The French aren't being entirely paranoid when they feel that their culture is under threat from America.

Consider this one statistic. Although the French take their cinema very seriously as an art form (Paris was the site of the first commercial screening of films for the public), four out of five French cinemas are now controlled by American film distributors.

There's a partial reason, but not a very good one, for Johnny Hallyday's success.

By government mandate, a minimum of 40 per cent of the air time devoted to popular music on national radio must be given over to French songs.

~~~~~

French schoolchildren have a head start on their contemporaries elsewhere.

French children begin their schooling at the age of three, in an *école maternelle*. This is followed, at six, by a year in an *école primaire*, then by two years in a *cours élémentaire* and two years in a *cours moyen*. At 11 the child enters a *collège* for four years, followed by another four years at a *lycée* – the last two of which are optional, but necessary if one plans to take the *Baccalauréat* (or *Bac*) examination and go on to university.

~~~~~

Pupils in France don't thank God it's Friday.

That's because French children go to school on Saturday mornings, and have Wednesdays off, although this practice has begun to change in favour of a Monday-to-Friday school week.

Unlike the UK or the US, France offers no social advantages to those attending a boarding school. Quite the reverse. Traditionally it's the naughty ones who get sent away to boarding school, where it's hoped they will learn about discipline. (This doesn't apply to children who live in remote parts of the country and have no choice but to attend a boarding school.)

The study of philosophy is still an important part of the school curriculum.

And as Descartes is the cornerstone of French philosophy, French intellectualism is marbled with Cartesian logic – which gives rise to the old joke about the Frenchman's typical approach to problem-solving: "It may work in practice, but will it work in theory?"

~~~~~

Universities are where the superb French educational system breaks down.

Anyone who passes the *Baccalauréat* can go to university, free, which means that most universities are overcrowded and underfunded. This in turn makes it difficult to recruit the best professors and lecturers, leading to a consequent drop in standards. Conditions at some institutions, including the venerable Sorbonne, are said to be so bad that they've reached 'Third World levels'.

The *grandes écoles*, on the other hand, are equal or superior to any institutions of higher learning anywhere in the world.

The *grandes écoles*, which are unique to France, are a group of some 500 elite academies which are much more demanding than the universities and infinitely harder to get into. Admission is by a set of extremely rigorous competitive exams, both written and oral, which can require two or three years of special preparatory study. Even then, only one in ten candidates will make it into the *grandes écoles* of their choice.

But those who do make it – especially the 110 who are admitted to the *Ecole Nationale d'Administration*, or *ENA* (known as *'énarques'*), the most prestigious of them all – know that it's only a matter of time before they're running the country. Thus a meritocratic process is used to create a privileged elite. But along with the privilege comes a duty to the country: any *énarque* who leaves public service for the private sector is referred to derisively as a *pantouflard* (slipper-wearer).

~~~~~

French schoolchildren are among the worst in Europe at learning English.

Or to put it another way, they're among the worst at being taught English. Whichever way one chooses to look at the problem, a report recently published in France said that French schoolchildren were falling so far behind their counterparts in other EU countries that it recommended that English be made compulsory in French schools from the age of eight onwards.

President Chirac responded by calling the spread of English at the expense of French "a disaster" (see **Chapter 3**).

~~~~~

The last word on the importance the French attach to their culture belongs to an angry drunk.

One night several years ago an English friend was having drinks alone in a Paris bar when he got into an argument with a Frenchman seated nearby. As the two got drunker, the argument got more heated, until finally the Frenchman stormed out in a blind rage. To this day my friend cannot recall what the argument was about, but he will never forget his antagonist's inspired parting shot: "I suppose now you're going to tell me that Rimbaud wasn't the greatest of poets!"

3.

SOME SURPRISING THINGS ABOUT THE
FRENCH LANGUAGE

Ever since 1635 when Cardinal Richelieu established the Académie Française to protect and defend the French language against mongrelisation by outside influences, the French have been vigilant in looking out for the purity of their mother tongue. This vigilance has been zealously practised by the *Académiciens* themselves, the 40 'Immortals' elected for life who are also charged with the task of laying down the rules – there must be rules – which have to be obeyed if crimes aren't to be committed against the language.

~~~~~

The Académie doesn't permit changes lightly.

The last major reform authorised by the Immortals which was enacted by legislation was the abandonment of the imperfect subjunctive early in the last century.

~~~~~

Even minor spelling changes can provoke seismic reactions.

The last time a (minor) spelling change was approved was in 1835. When in 1990 the Académie considering abolishing the circumflex on certain words, it caused a national uproar. Everyone took part in the debate; distinguished public figures, authors, diplomats, even Nobel Prizewinners wrote Letters to the Editor. The issue dominated the headlines, pushing the first Gulf War off the front pages. In the end, the idea was quietly dropped.

~~~~~

English is the French bête noire.

For the past half-century the main preoccupation of the Académie has been the struggle to roll back the tide of English expressions that threatens to engulf French. The original impetus behind this campaign came, in the '60s, from Quebec, where 6 million French Canadians found themselves marooned in a sea of 300 million English-speakers. The French government responded by establishing, in 1966, the *Haut Comité de la Langue Française*, whose job it was to create French words and phrases to replace the English ones that had infiltrated the language of France. As this met with only limited success, a law was passed in 1974 making it obligatory to provide a translation of all foreign words and phrases used in advertisements.

And now the country's broadcasting authority, the CSA, has called on French television and radio stations to use French titles for such popular French shows as 'Star Academy'. This prompted the newspaper *Libération* to ask, tongue in cheek, whether 'Loft Story' would now be catchily known as *Une histoire de local à usage commercial ou industriel aménagé en local d'habitation*.

This would seem to be a lost cause, judging by the growing number of English words commonly used by the French. Here are only a few that one finds in everyday use (they're all masculine):

Badge	*Barbecue*
Best-seller	*Blue-jean*
Blues	*Bluff*
Box-office	*Bulldozer*
Bungalow	*Call-girl*
Car ferry	*Club*
Cocktail	*Cover-girl*
Dancing	*Design*
Detective	*Discount*
Doping	*Escalator*
Fair-play	*Fan*
Fast-food	*Feedback*
Gadget	*Gangster*

Gay	*Gentleman*
Hall	*Handicap*
Hit-parade	*Hold-up*
Hooligan	*Jogging*
Kidnapping	*Kit*
Knock-out	*Leader*
Look	*Magazine*
Manager	*Marketing*
Mass-media	*Music-hall*
Name-dropping	*One-man-show*
Pacemaker	*Parking*
Pickpocket	*Pin-up*
Planning	*Playback*
Play-boy	*Puzzle*
Scoop	*Self-made-man*
Self-service	*Sex-appeal*
Show business	*Slogan*
Snob	*Software*
Sponsoring	*Star/starlet*
Steack (sic)	*Stress*
Supporter	*Sweatshirt*
Time-sharing	*Week-end*

And of course there are reminders of the spread of English all over France in the shape of STOP signs.

~~~~~

The biggest joke ever played on the Académie Française was the work of IBM.

In 1954 IBM was trying to popularise the use of computers around the world. Although the word 'computer', or some variation on it, presented no problem in other languages, the marketing people at

IBM were aware of French sensitivities regarding imported words. Moreover, they felt that the first syllable of 'computer' came perilously close to the obscene word *con*, while *pute* was French for 'whore'. So with the best of intentions they came up with the trademark term *ordinateur*, which was officially adopted as the correct generic term a decade or so later. So while the rest of the world works away on its computers – by a further irony, the principal instrument for the global spread of English – the French are stuck with their American-named *ordinateurs*.

~~~~~

French is the only major language in the world that is spoken more widely as a second language than as a first language.

It's also the only language apart from English that is spoken on every continent.

~~~~~

French has fewer words than you think.

English, for example, has over 20,000 words in everyday use, whereas French has only 6,000. More tellingly, the entire *oeuvre* of Racine, France's greatest tragedian, uses only around 3,000 words.

~~~~~

The great strengths of French are also its weaknesses.

The nuances and subtle ambiguities that made French the perfect language of international diplomacy also make it ill-suited to the wheeling and dealing of international commerce. Likewise, the built-in formality that makes the language invaluable in the fine-tuning of relationships can be off-putting in a world of psychobabble where everyone is on first-name terms with everyone else.

Having a relatively small vocabulary compared with English may mean that French is mercifully free from swarms of synonyms or ugly neologisms, but also in many cases it guarantees a degree of imprecision that would be unacceptable in English. And the fact that it's governed by strict rules, which accounts for its elegant combination of logic and eloquence, gives it an inflexibility that makes it difficult for it to adapt to a world that is changing faster than it is.

~~~~~

The worst insult of all to the French language was delivered by the European Union.

In July 2002 the European Union ruled that all product labels in the EU should be in English. French foods labelled in English? *C'est con*!

~~~~~

French has now dropped out of the top ten of the most spoken languages.

This may be shocking news to French-speakers, but worse is yet to come. Some language experts predict that in the near future only five languages will have any sort of global currency: English, Mandarin, Spanish, Russian, and Arabic. (This list is doubly wounding to the French because not only does it give top ranking to English, but it also includes Spanish, a favourite butt of French ridicule.) Although Mandarin has easily the world's largest number of speakers, this is due to the fecundity of the Chinese rather than the serviceability of their language. English, on the other hand, in addition to being the language of the world's last great empire as well as its only current superpower, with its 'cultural imperialism', also happens to be the language of the internet. There's simply no hiding from it.

~~~~~

Conversation in French gets easier the further you get from Paris.

This may be metaphorically rather than geographically true, but it's a state of affairs that the majority of French themselves would recognise. For one thing, Parisians tend to elide words into one another, so that the listener is often left unpicking syllables long after they've been uttered. For another thing, when one is speaking to Parisians they often display a level of incomprehension that can only come with practice.

People from rural France – who for the most part cordially detest Parisians – frequently complain of both characteristics. But it was the latter that drew the humorous fire of Mark Twain over a century ago: "In Paris, they simply stared when I spoke to them in French; I never did succeed in making those idiots understand their own language."

~~~~~

French postmen can be depended on to help you learn the language.

That's because they can be depended on to deposit in your letter box   stacks of advertising leaflets and circulars from local merchants, supermarkets, department stores, etc. full of photographs of the goods on sale – making them handy as illustrated dictionaries.

In French, an 'o' in time will save you time.

It's worth knowing that quite a few French words in common usage are regularly abbreviated by lopping off the final syllable or two and substituting an 'o'. Probably the best known example is the *apéro* (aperitif).

Here are some more:

alcolo	alcoholic
aristo	aristocrat
chrono	stopwatch
coco	communist
collabo	collaborator
croco	crocodile skin
dico	dictionary
écolo	ecologist
édito	editorial
facho	fascist
frigo	fridge
géo	geography
intello	intellectual
invalo	invalid
labo	laboratory
maso	masochist
mégalo	megalomaniac
météo	weather forecast
parano	paranoid
porno	porno
prolo	proletarian
proprio	proprietor, owner
socialo	socialist
toxico	drug addict

The simplest words cause the most confusion.

As the above selection would suggest, many French words have close relatives in English; as the selection below will show, one can get into trouble assuming that there are any identical twins in the two languages.

Not long ago some bright spark put forward the theory that most words of three syllables or more in French have the same meaning as in English. While it's certainly true that a large number of words in both languages have the same spelling, give or take an accent here and there, one should be very careful about using them interchangeably, because French is infested with *faux amis* (false friends) that can make you look very foolish indeed if you use them improperly.

I will begin with some of the verbs that cause the most confusion:

assister	to attend
attirer	to attract, entice
commander	to order (as a meal)
contrôler	to check, verify
demander	to ask (not demand)
passer un examen	to take (not pass) a test
réaliser	to create
retirer	to take off, remove

And then there's the too-versatile *apprendre*, which can mean either 'to learn' or 'to teach'.

Some nouns:

avertissement	warning
bon	slip, form, coupon

caméra	a video or movie camera only
car	bus, coach
courtier	broker
déception	disappointment
étiquette	ticket, label
forfait	set price
location	renting, letting
monnaie	change (coins)
occasion	second-hand buy, bargain
plaisanterie	joke
publicité	advertising
raisin	grape
sinistre	accident, disaster

And a few adjectives:

ancien	old, former, ex-
extra	first-rate, terrific
génial	inspired, brilliant
rentable	profitable
sensible	sensitive

These are the words that must be handled with care, if not avoided altogether.

The first is another false friend: *queue*. Although it can have the same meaning as in English, it's principally defined as a tail, stem, or stalk – which inevitably means that it moonlights as a crude slang word for phallus.

But undoubtedly the trickiest is *baiser* because it's both an innocent noun meaning 'kiss' and an incendiary verb meaning 'to f***'. Thus, *bons baisers* translates, sweetly, as 'love and kisses', whereas *elle baise bien* means . . . well, you get the idea.

4.

SOME SURPRISING THINGS ABOUT
FRENCH HISTORY

One of the most often repeated lines among Francophobes trying to be funny is the one about how wonderful France would be if it weren't for the French. This may be feeble as humour goes, but as history goes it's abject nonsense. The French have always been there, or at least as far back into prehistory as we can trace.

Unlike the inhabitants of other lands, whose ancestors were deposited there by one of the waves of human migration, the French are their own native people.

~~~~~

The French may also have been the first Americans.

When DNA tests were done on the earliest known human bones ever found in North America, the results matched those of tests carried out on 20,000-year-old bones found in the Bordeaux region of France.

As the polar ice cap extended as far south as Bordeaux during the last Ice Age, it would have been possible to cross the Atlantic ice along the ocean's edge, where fish would have been in plentiful supply.

~~~~~

For a thousand years the French monarchy ruled only Paris.

Although the first 'King of France' was the Frankish chieftain Clovis, who was crowned and baptised by St Rémy at Reims in 481, it wasn't until the end of the 15th century, with the annexation of Brittany and Burgundy, that the royal writ ran beyond the Ile de France area around Paris.

Although the Crusades were meant to secure the Holy Land for Christianity, one was launched against the French.

Between the Fourth Crusade and the Children's Crusade, Pope Innocent III in 1208 initiated a bloody crusade against the Cathars of south-west France, whose unorthodox beliefs were regarded as heretical. The Cathar 'heresy' was crushed at a cost of thousands of lives.

~~~~~

The Marseillaise should really be called the Strasbourgeoise.

When Captain Claude Rouget de Lisle composed the national anthem in 1792, he was garrisoned in Strasbourg. After it was sung by the Marseille National Guard on entering Paris later that year, it became known as the *Marseillaise*.

~~~~~

The French were the original saboteurs.

Wooden clogs, or *sabots*, were worn by the French before they were taken up by the Dutch. As they became identified with clumsiness and messy work, they gave their name to sabotage.

~~~~~

Even the national emblem of France is a jeu de mots.

The rooster that is emblematic of the French Republic first appeared on the bell towers of churches after the Revolution, greeting the new dawn. It was adopted as France's national emblem under the Second

Republic (1848–52). There's a widespread suspicion, however, that it's in fact a 2,000-year-old visual pun, as the Latin word for France, *Gallus* (or 'Gaul'), also means 'rooster'. Wags like to point out that the rooster characteristically crows loudly and pointlessly, while remaining aloof from the other animals in the barnyard.

~~~~~

France once enjoyed the distinction of having a saint for a king.

Louis IX, who reigned from 1226 to 1270, was canonised in 1296, becoming St Louis.

~~~~~

'Marianne', the symbolic personification of the French Republic, actually had a religious background.

Although the name Marianne was chosen simply because it was the most popular woman's name at the time of the Revolution and thus had impeccable credentials as representative of the masses, the name itself was a combination of the names of the Virgin Mary and St Anne. This was tacitly if unwittingly acknowledged by the revolutionary mobs who stormed through the streets chanting, in a tasteless parody of the *Ave Maria*, "Hail Marianne, full of strength, the People are with thee; Blessed is the fruit of thy womb, the Republic".

~~~~~

The French state has been all but erased from history.

France as a state is always known as the *République Française*, and the initials RF are engraved above the front doors of government buildings throughout France. The total abolition of the word 'State' (*État*) from official usage is due to the fact that *État Française* was the title used by the collaborationist Vichy regime in World War II.

~~~~~

Bart Simpson wasn't entirely original when he insulted the French.

Bart was actually being a clever anthologist when he coined his famous phrase, "cheese-eating surrender monkeys", to describe the French. In 1951, an exasperated Charles de Gaulle had already asked, "How can you govern a country which has 246 varieties of cheese?" During the Napoleonic Wars the English troops' slang term for a Frenchman was Jimmy Rend – from *Je me rends*, I surrender. And the great Voltaire himself once referred to his compatriots as "idle monkeys".

~~~~~

The guillotine was introduced as an instrument of equal rights.

A physician and member of the National Assembly after the Revolution, Dr Joseph Guillotin was so offended by the different ways that the rich and the poor were executed under the *ancien régime* that he proposed a means of decapitation for everyone to ensure social justice for the condemned. Forty thousand severed heads later, he regretted that such an efficient means of execution had fallen into the hands of such an enthusiastic executioner as Robespierre.

Dr Guillotin devoted his last years to the introduction of vaccination against smallpox and the abolition of slavery. The guillotine was retired when capital punishment was abolished by President Mitterrand in 1981.

France is a country built for warfare.

All those wonders of the French landscape that attract tourists in their millions today – the mighty castles with their moats and drawbridges, the turreted chateaux rising splendidly out of the forests, the hilltop villages and walled towns – were originally built, lest we forget, to repel invaders.

~~~~~

The Hundred Years War was only incidentally a conflict between England and France.

For most of its duration it was a series of family squabbles over territory. It was only after the Battle of Agincourt in 1415, which effectively ended feudalism and ushered in the era of the nation state and the professional army, that it broadened into an Anglo-French conflict. Despite the English victory at Agincourt, the French went on to win the war.

~~~~~

Joan of Arc wasn't executed for heresy or sorcery.

In reality, the English had her burnt at the stake for humiliating them in battle while dressed as a man. It was the cross-dressing that got to them. How times change.

~~~~~

Not only the French were defeated at Agincourt.

The whole ideal of chivalry, which the French had invented, died out with the invention of the longbow, against which the French knight (or *chevalier*) was powerless. It could truly be said that the longbow delivered the final slap in the face to chivalry, inasmuch as a young Frenchman was created a *chevalier* not by a tap on the shoulder with a sword but with a slap across the face, to signify the last time he would receive a blow without responding.

~~~~~

Haute couture was invented by an Englishman.

Charles Worth, an Englishman who had settled in Paris, founded the first *maison de haute couture* there in 1858.

~~~~~

The concept of 'left' and 'right' in politics originated in France.

After the Revolution, monarchists sat to the right and republicans to the left of the President of the National Assembly.

~~~~~

The French were driving cars and flying machines as early as the 18th century.

The first steam carriage was built by Nicolas-Joseph Cugnot in 1769, and the first manned flight was by the Montgolfier brothers in their balloon in 1783. Jean Etienne Lenoir patented the first internal combustion engine in 1860, leading directly to the establishment of the car industry. Indeed, the word *automobile* itself is French, which will no doubt come as a shock to George W. Bush, who once memorably told Tony Blair that the French had no word for *entrepreneur*.

5.

SOME SURPRISING THINGS ABOUT
FRENCH MANNERS

Ever since the middle of the 14th century, when chivalry was in flower, Europeans have subscribed to the proverb that 'manners maketh man'. Only the French, however, took it seriously enough to construct a protocol that prescribed the appropriate behaviour.

~~~~~

Even criminal activity falls within the purview of the rules of etiquette.

Indeed, to fail to come to the aid of someone who has been the victim of a crime is itself a crime.

~~~~~

You should always greet someone with 'Bonjour' or 'Bonsoir'.

And always add *'Monsieur'* or *'Madame'*. It isn't enough to extend a half-greeting; it needs to be personalised, even if formally. Beyond that, the form of the greeting depends on the level of familiarity: *'Bonjour, Monsieur Lacaze'*; *'Bonsoir, Marie'*, etc.

When there are too many people to acknowledge individually, such as in a shop, a collective greeting is acceptable: *'Bonjour, Mesdames, Messieurs'*. However, it isn't acceptable, unless you're making a joke with friends, to telescope a greeting into the standard shopkeeper's contraction: *'Bonjour, Messieurs-dames'*.

On being introduced to someone for the first time, it used to be correct to say *'Enchanté'*. Not that it's incorrect now, but it's considered somewhat old-fashioned and affected. Still, better to be old-fashioned than chummy. In France, it's always preferable to err on the side of formality.

Most greetings are incomplete without a handshake.

Whenever you open the door to a tradesman or salesman, or are invited to meet someone, or show up for work, or attend a party, or bump into an acquaintance in the street, handshakes are expected. They aren't obligatory, but failure to observe this minimal courtesy will be taken as a signal of the symbolic distance you wish to keep between yourself and others. Even workmen with dirty hands will extend a forearm to be gripped rather than risk the rudeness of withholding a handshake.

By the way, it's also considered impolite to talk with your hands in your pockets.

~~~~~

Social kissing isn't as simple as you might think.

As social kisses come from the vocabulary of manners rather than of personal intimacy, they follow a more complicated set of rules. The first problem is whom to kiss. Obviously all friends come into this category, plus their children and (usually) their parents. Then come those people with whom you're on friendly terms, or whom you have known a long time, or whom you see regularly at dinner parties or other social occasions.

So far, so good. But then there are those situations where for some obscure reason different combinations apply: where men shake hands and the women kiss, for example, or where the women kiss and the men kiss the women but shake hands with each other. In these situations, when in doubt the best tactic is to delay for a split second while you decide whether the other person is leading with a cheek or a hand. If it isn't immediately obvious which, just shake hands. You won't lose any points for diffidence, but you will for over-familiarity. Besides, if you sense that you've been too undemonstrative, you can always make amends on leave-taking at the end of the occasion – or the next time.

~~~~~

You should never kiss once.

This is almost a theological matter, of the same order as speculations regarding angels and pinheads. As a rule, you can bestow any number of kisses between two and four in Paris, while it's usually three in the rest of the country. It depends on what is customary in any given area. But it's never, anywhere, just one kiss (except with small children).

The ritual is usually conducted in the following sequence: right cheek to right cheek, left to left, right to right, etc. There are exceptions, of course, but you can spot them in advance by holding back momentarily to see which way the other person goes. That way, should they unexpectedly incline in the wrong direction, you won't end up shadow-boxing or head-butting. If you're bespectacled, it's also a good idea to remove your glasses beforehand to avoid locking antlers with the other person.

~~~~~

In speaking or writing, don't use the familiar forms of address until it's proper to do so.

Formality is built into the language for a reason. It defines the nature of one's relationships. When you're invited to abandon the *vous* form for the more familiar *tu*, or when it's otherwise made clear that such familiarity would no longer be presumptuous, you know that the relationship has passed an important milestone.

Likewise, albeit less significantly, the discarding of *Monsieur* or *Madame* in favour of first names marks a transitional stage in one's dealings with others. (If those dealings are primarily professional, even this comparatively early stage may never be reached.)

In the salutations that open letters, the road to familiarity is even more carefully signposted, as one progresses from *Monsieur*, to *Cher Monsieur*, to *Cher Monsieur Dupont*, to *Cher Pierre*, to *Mon cher Pierre*.

If you're ever tempted to think that this whole *tu/vous* business isn't serious, consider the case of the Parisian barrister who was arrested in early 2005 for various offences committed on his motor scooter. When he was taken to the police station, he not only had to suffer the indignity of being handcuffed to a radiator, but the officers had the nerve to address him as *tu*. He immediately filed a suit claiming police brutality.

~~~~~

When a couple enters a building, the man goes first.

As with the convention that calls for the man to walk outside the woman on the pavement, there are various explanations of the origin of this ritualised habit. Whichever one happens to be true, the man still goes through the door first and, if necessary, holds it open for the woman from the inside.

~~~~~

Cosmetic self-improvement isn't a proper outdoor activity.

At the risk of appearing to discriminate harshly against Italians, the French disapprove of men combing their hair in the street. Similarly, women are frowned upon who apply their make-up in public.

Never telephone between noon and 3pm on a Sunday.

This is perhaps the most special time of the week, when families get together for Sunday lunch. In fact, unless it's an emergency, one should hold off phoning till after 5pm, as a post-prandial nap is often on the Sunday agenda.

On the other hand, while it's inconsiderate to interrupt anyone's mealtime, often the period between noon and 2pm on weekdays is the only time you can be sure of catching people such as plumbers or electricians who don't have mobile phones.

~~~~~

It's acceptable to open a closed door unbidden.

That is, provided you knock first. Knocking announces your intention and there's no need to wait for an answer before entering.

~~~~~

Certain gifts are more welcome than others.

Excellent chocolates from a *chocolatier artisanal* are always welcome, as is a good vintage Champagne, whether you're bringing gifts as a dinner guest or a house guest. Wine is problematical, unless you have a couple of bottles of a truly sensational wine that you want to share with special friends who will appreciate it; otherwise, you risk insulting your hosts with the implied suggestion that they're incapable of choosing the right wine to go with their own meal, or that, whatever they've chosen, your choice is likely to be superior.

Flowers, too, are encoded with a message other than "Thank you for inviting us". Chrysanthemums, for instance, signify death and are usually reserved for family graves at *Toussaint* (All Saints' Day). Carnations are thought to bring bad luck, while yellow flowers often carry unhappy associations with cuckoldry. Red roses are always safe, as are daffodils, lilies and tulips in the spring.

~~~~~

It's bad luck to wish someone good luck.

Don't ask. It just is.

~~~~~

Eye contact can send unintended signals.

This is a tricky one. Staring at passers-by in the road, unsettling as it can be to those who are being stared at, is considered perfectly all right. Indeed, it's almost ill-mannered not to stare: it shows that you aren't really interested in the people passing by. If you don't care enough to stare, you're probably a foreigner, or a Parisian.

On the other hand, if you look directly into someone's eyes in the street or in a café, it will probably be taken as either challenging or flirtatious, usually the latter. Yet a refusal to make eye contact with someone – especially someone in a serving role – is considered an act of snobbery, a put-down.

~~~~~

Even in a land where the national sport is conversation, there are some taboo subjects.

Foremost among these are 'personal' topics. You don't ask someone's name, or age, or income, or what they do for a living. The exception is almost any question about a person's health, which will often call forth a torrent of unwanted information and will sooner or later involve a discussion of the liver or digestive tract – or both.

By contrast, any subject – the more controversial, the better – that invites an opinion is blessed. The French cherish any opportunity to express their opinions on things they care about. This means, above all, anything to do with politics, history, philosophy, art and literature, food and wine. On matters of such import, everyone is expected to have an opinion and to be ready to fight their corner, to argue, to dispute, to interrupt, to contradict: it all contributes to the liveliness, and therefore the success, of the conversation.

The only serious *faux pas* one can make in a good conversation, apart from wanting to change the subject to the weather, is to profess ignorance of the matter being discussed or to claim not to have any opinion about it; this won't be seen as engaging humility but as rank arrogance, a refusal to treat the conversation as worthy of your participation.

~~~~~

The French don't smile readily, for a good reason.

Or, more precisely, they only smile when they have a good reason. To the French, indiscriminate smiling at people they don't know is, except among imbeciles who can't help it, a display of the worst sort of hypocrisy. You smile at someone who has amused you, or pleased you, or made you happy; if they haven't, you don't. It's as simple as that. As the French see it, if one is going to treat both friends and strangers to the same facial expression, one might as well just paint on a clown's face in the morning; it would be equally meaningless.

The above doesn't apply to dogs: the French are always happy for you to smile at their dogs.

~~~~~

There's a special form of queuing in France.

To the casual observer, a French queue bears closer resemblance to an improvised game of tag than to an orderly sequence. There is, however, an invisible line that can be drawn between the people dotted round a shop waiting to be served. It isn't a straight line, as that would be an affront to the innate French need to be the exception to every rule. Instead, the line zigzags through the memory of the shopkeeper, who in most cases has remembered whose turn it is, and is generally scrupulous about attending to his customers in the proper order. It should also be said that, in my experience, the customers themselves are happy to defer to those with a prior claim on a shopkeeper's attention.

~~~~~

The French are never to blame for anything.

They may have been mistaken, they may have committed an error, but they must not be blamed. So whenever you find yourself tempted to assign blame, remember: it isn't their fault!

Admittedly, this sounds like a delinquent's charter, but in truth it sums up an eminently sensible approach to the problem of things gone wrong. Unlike the Englishman who bumps into you and automatically says, "Sorry", a Frenchman might crash into you repeatedly while you were parked and just as automatically refuse to accept that he was at fault. This isn't simply a way of shifting the blame; it's rather more profound than that. It's a way of shifting the focus away from the whole concept of blame and on to the issue of how to correct the problem, how to put things right. Of course it's the sophist's way of shirking responsibility, but it's also the realist's way of moving more quickly towards a solution.

~~~~~

You shouldn't be late for lunch.

The French, like most Mediterranean peoples, aren't particularly concerned about punctuality. On the other hand, they do care about their lunchtime, so any time that is lost in being late for lunch is time stolen from the most important meal of the day.

~~~~~

'Keep the change' doesn't translate into French.

If you're given money to buy something for somebody, always return the exact amount left unspent. Likewise, never refuse the change from a purchase made on your behalf, however inconsequential the sum. The French don't like having relationships spoiled by such vulgar considerations as money owed.

~~~~~

No one is exempt from the requirement to establish one's debating credentials.

Even lovers or married couples are expected to argue, often heatedly, in public. It's a sure sign of passion and strength of commitment. Couples who invariably agree with each other, or are quick to compromise, create an impression not of blissful togetherness but of boredom and indifference.

In business dealings, get slowly to the point.

Any financial or commercial transaction in France will proceed more smoothly if you take the scenic route to the bottom line. Directness in negotiating is seen as a form of brusqueness and isn't appreciated. It's also considered better manners to proffer your business card at the conclusion of a meeting, as the French do, rather than at the beginning.

~~~~~

French formality stops short of written thanks.

After a dinner party, for example, the French will thank you for the evening, adding a complimentary flourish about the meal if they feel they've eaten particularly well. And indeed they may telephone you the next day to reinforce their gratitude. But they don't send 'thank you' notes. The same goes for gifts: the thanks will be oral, and on the spot. After that, the gift (or meal) may become a conversational reference point but it won't become the subject of a formal acknowledgment.

Sometimes even spoken thanks will be assumed rather than expressed. When offered a second helping of food, for instance, *'Non'* means 'No, thank you'. *'Non, merci'*, which would come more naturally to polite English-speakers, in fact means 'No – yes', as if you've changed your mind in mid-reply, whereas *'Merci'* on its own frequently means 'No'.

So the quality of *merci* is strained by circumstances. But where manners are concerned, it's still better to be confusing while trying to be polite than to be impolite while trying to be exact.

6.

SOME SURPRISING THINGS ABOUT
FRENCH POLITICS

What is still more amazing than the grotesque amount of corruption that exists at the highest levels of the French government is the apparent willingness of the French electorate to tolerate their corrupt officials – indeed, to keep electing them. Think about it. The ethically-challenged Giscard d'Estaing was succeeded by the scandal-spattered François Mitterrand, who was re-elected before being replaced at the Elysée Palace by the egregious Jacques Chirac, who in 1999 wisely obtained a ruling from the constitutional council that extended the President's immunity from prosecution to cover offences he may have committed before taking office.

~~~~~

The French economy is booming.

Either the fourth or fifth largest economy in the world, depending on whose figures you prefer to believe, it's unarguably the fastest growing in Europe.

~~~~~

The French economy is in trouble.

The 35-hour week, which was meant to create jobs, has succeeded only in creating a culture of indifference to work and, in labour-intensive industries, a huge burden of extra costs. Meanwhile, output per head has fallen by 5 per cent. Although French workers typically enjoy an annual bonus equivalent to an extra month's pay, plus up to five weeks' paid holiday every year, the average employee costs his company double what he receives in remuneration, thanks to the massive social security contributions employers are obliged to make on behalf of their employees. The insurance giant AXA, for example, pays more to the state for its workers than it does to its workers in wages.

Moreover, government regulations make it very difficult to fire employees, while the obstructive state bureaucracy makes it equally difficult to start a business of one's own. Only 6 per cent of the French workforce is self-employed. As a result, France is economically one of the least competitive among developed nations.

~~~~~

The Americanisation of French electoral politics has begun in earnest.

It started when the French abandoned their long-observed custom of keeping the private lives of public officials strictly private. However, once the door was opened to public scrutiny, the politicians quickly seized on the opportunity to use the media in the political marketing of their families. Now, as in the US, more and more candidates come as part of a political package that includes happy, smiling family members.

~~~~~

There's a remarkable fondness for going on strike in France.

There are two principal reasons for this. The first is historical: ever since the Revolution, the French have had an honoured tradition of taking to the streets to make their feelings known. So there's an instinctive tolerance, not to say sympathy, for strikers even when their public *manifestations* cause inconvenience.

The second reason is broadly philosophical. The French are happy to grant the government the right to lay claim to large chunks of their income to finance its welfare programmes, and at the same time to cede vast regulatory powers to the bureaucracy to implement these programmes, but they expect a *quid pro quo* in the form of excellent public services and guaranteed job security. By and large, this social contract works well, and few would consider dismantling it, but when it does break down the French are quick to remind the government of its side of the bargain.

Even so, the occasional noisy march or blockade notwithstanding, there's a decidedly ho-hum quality to most French strikes and protest demonstrations. This is partly because strikes and demos are more for the purpose of making a point than causing economic damage. In fact, far fewer working days are lost annually through industrial action in France than in Britain or, proportionately, the US. And demonstrations are seldom disruptive because newspapers publish the details in advance, showing which roads will be blocked between which times. In Paris, for instance, *Le Parisien* publishes the day's schedule of demos next to the weather forecast.

~~~~~

The government has a novel way of settling the more embarrassing strikes.

First of all, the government announces that it will take a hard line against the strikers. If the strike involves outdoor confrontations, this can mean calling out the *CRS*, the fearsome state security police, in full riot gear. This is a well rehearsed step in the war dance. There have been times when strike leaders have been secretly annoyed when the government failed to call out the *CRS*, because it gave the impression that the government wasn't taking them seriously. The next step is for the government to effect a settlement by quietly giving in to all of the strikers' demands. The final step is for the government to hail the new settlement and then proceed to ignore it until the next strike.

The French pension system is headed for meltdown.

When Louis XIV built the *Invalides* as a hostel for disabled soldiers, it was one of the world's first pension schemes. Now the system that grew out of this pioneering state benefit looks like becoming disabled itself. With only 38 per cent of men aged 55 to 64 working, the lowest percentage in Europe, France now has only three workers per pensioner, a ratio that is expected to drop to two to one by 2030 if drastic action isn't taken.

~~~~~

There are no juries in France.

The jury of one's peers was abolished in 1941 and replaced by a tribunal consisting of nine judges – six ordinary citizens and three professional judges. In criminal cases, the presiding magistrate has a more inquisitorial function than in other countries, usually conducting most of the questioning of witnesses.

~~~~~

The real power in French politics is at the top – or at the bottom.

Despite the Revolution, and intermittent efforts at decentralisation ever since, political power in France remains concentrated in the hands of a few, at the national level. France's 37,000 *communes* are spread across 96 *départements*, which are in turn clustered into 22 administrative *régions*. Although the country can boast one elected local councillor for every 110 voters, compared with one for every 1,800 voters in Britain, there's no local autonomy or sovereignty, and no competing political jurisdictions, as there are in the UK and the US. The *départements* and *régions* in effect function merely as arms of the state, with no real independence.

On the other hand, the mayor of even the smallest village or hamlet has considerable power in matters of importance to the average citizen, such as granting building permits, acting as *de facto* police chief, making environmental decisions, overseeing local schools and social services, performing marriages, and a whole range of other responsibilities depending on the size of the community. Up to a point – the point at which a village becomes dependent on a nearby commune for its services – it's mayors who have the greatest power in terms of their ability to have a direct influence on people's lives. By this reckoning, the least powerful mayor in France is probably the mayor of Paris (a post that didn't exist from 1871 to 1977). The mayor of Paris doesn't even have power over the city's police or public transport. The real municipal power, such as it is, rests with the mayors of Paris's 20 *arrondissements*.

~~~~~

The most important public official in French life is probably the notary.

Anything to do with property – buying or selling it, leasing or transferring it – requires (by law) the services of a *notaire*. Likewise, matters concerning testamentary acts, wills, divorces, loans, taxes or setting up a business usually need a *notaire*. If in any doubt, consult a *notaire*.

~~~~~

Some things never change.

At the birth of the First Republic over 200 years ago, the writer Sébastien Chamfort, himself a Jacobin revolutionary, observed: "If it were not for the government, we should have nothing left to laugh at in France."

7.

SOME SURPRISING THINGS ABOUT

FRENCH
FOOD & DRINK

Whatever you've been told about French food and drink, it's probably true – or has been true at some time – even when it appears to contradict something else you've been told. This happens when a nation is in thrall to its taste buds.

~~~~~

To the French, great cuisine ranks with great works of art and philosophy among the highest achievements of civilisation.

Cynics will see this merely as exalting self-indulgence, a way of making gluttony respectable, whereas in truth it's a celebration of the intellect's ability to tame the animal appetite, and at the same time to educate it in ways that would have been impossible by a simple surrender to hunger.

~~~~~

French fries aren't a Belgian invention.

Diehard believers in this popular myth are directed to the writings of Thomas Jefferson, in which references can be found to "Potatoes Fried in the French Manner" 30 years before Belgium existed as a country.

~~~~~

France has the highest level of wine consumption (per person over 14) of any country in the world, but not for much longer.

French drinkers each consume 58 litres of wine a year, the British 16 and the Americans only eight. Nevertheless, just 40 years ago the French were getting through more than 100 litres annually, and the figure is continuing to fall. In 1980, there were 37 'occasional' drinkers for every 100 'regular' drinkers. Now the occasional drinkers outnumber the regulars by almost two to one, and a third of all adults drink no wine at all. No wonder there are alarm bells tolling in the vineyards.

~~~~~

Mineral water isn't mineral water until the Ministry of Health says so.

While there are dozens of brands of bottled spring water available in France, no brand can be labelled *eau minérale* until the Ministry of Health is satisfied that it has genuinely therapeutic properties – or at least until the Ministry feels that it has had a therapeutic effect on the liquidity of those employed to pass judgement on it.

~~~~~

France's main tinned food is cassoulet.

There are at least half a dozen popular varieties on sale. The dish comes from the south-west, where, despite its peasant origins in the Middle Ages, it's taken very seriously indeed. There's even a *Grande Confrérie du Cassoulet*, based in Castelnaudary, with around 1,000 members presided over by a grand master, all dedicated to the preservation of the centuries-old method of making *cassoulet*.

The dish on which so much love and energy is lavished derives its name from the *cassole*, the glazed terracotta bowl in which it's cooked, and it consists of white kidney beans and, well, just about anything else you want to throw in the pot: stock, lamb, pork, chicken, veal, duck, Toulouse sausages, vegetables, herbs, garlic, onions . . . There are as many different recipes as there are people who have cooked it. But however it comes, it remains the perfect meal for a cold winter's day.

~~~~~

France is a vegetarian's paradise.

Local markets – and every town has one – are justly valued for the splendid variety and quality of their fresh vegetables, fruit, herbs, spices, plants, nuts, and so on. As such, they're ideal hunting grounds for vegetarians.

Which is just as well, because restaurants aren't. Although vegetarians are no longer treated by restaurateurs and café owners as if they were guilty of some unspeakable crime against nature, they're still seen by many as having only been released on a technicality. As for vegans, they're too weird to bother getting upset about, rather like Zoroastrians or Elvis impersonators.

~~~~~

The French aren't especially keen on frogs' legs.

As far as they're concerned, frogs' legs are just another item on the menu – and not every menu at that. Their assumed taste for frogs' legs came about because the French can – and do – make use of anything in the preparation of food. No part of a plant or animal goes unused. Therefore we tend to pay particular attention to those things that we would never have thought of eating ourselves, like bits of frogs.

That said, it must be admitted that there's sufficient demand for these bits among the French that they have to import 200 million frogs annually. But that's nothing compared to the 40,000 tons of snails they put away every year.

In any case, many foreigners' perception of French tastes is based not on what the French like but on what they themselves think they wouldn't like. Jeremy Clarkson disagrees; he says it's all a question of aesthetics. "The French hate anything that's ugly," he argues, concluding: "If they see an animal that's ugly, they immediately eat it."

~~~~~

One of our most familiar contemporary slogans was first formulated in a French kitchen almost 200 years ago.

Shortly before he died in 1826, the great French gourmet Anthelme Brillat-Savarin came up with the arresting notion that "you are what you eat".

~~~~~

The Appelation d'Origine Contrôlée (AOC) now applies to some foods as well as wine.

All bottled wines in France which meet certain standards and come from a designated area using specific grapes carry the government's *AOC* label, which in theory at least prevents inferior wines, or wines originating elsewhere, from being marketed misleadingly. The regulations are strict, and apply to around half of all the bottled wine produced in France. The success of the scheme in protecting producers and consumers alike has led to its extension to food products. The first such product to be granted an *AOC* was Roquefort cheese. Others now having an *AOC* include nuts from Grenoble, green lentils from Le Puy, olive oil from Les Baux-de-

Provence, potatoes from the Ile de Ré in the Atlantic, and poultry from Bresse, east of Lyon.

~~~~~

Cognac and Armagnac are separated by more than just geography.

Although Cognac and Armagnac are both famous brandies, and come from areas just north and south respectively of Bordeaux near France's southern Atlantic coast, they're much further apart than the geography would suggest.

For one thing, Armagnac has been produced in Gascony since the 13th century, some 400 years before Cognac first appeared in Charente. For another, it involves a single distillation whereas Cognac is distilled twice.

The equipment used is different, too, as Armagnac is distilled in an alembic, a type of still brought to France by the Moors, who originally tried to use it to turn lead into gold – a different sort of alchemy altogether.

Finally, while the production of Armagnac was very much a Gascon enterprise, many of the great Cognac-producing families were anything but Charentais: the Martells came from Jersey, the Hines from Dorset, and the Hennessys from Ireland, to name but three.

~~~~~

The French drink more whisky than brandy.

Twelve times more, to be exact. France is the second-largest market for whisky in the world.

The French would rather die than have to cook foreign food.

All right, that's an exaggeration. But it isn't as much of one as you might think. You only have to peer down the supermarket aisle which has the shelves marked *Saveurs ailleurs* ('Flavours from other places') or something similar, and contemplate the looks of uncomprehending horror on the faces of the people who have paused there, to realise how traumatised they must be at the thought of swallowing some foreigner's idea of a yummy treat.

And it becomes even less of an exaggeration when you consider the tragic case of Bernard Loiseau. Monsieur Loiseau was the internationally celebrated chef at La Côte d'Or in Saulieu, west of Dijon, which for 13 years running won the maximum three Michelin stars. Then, a few years ago, foreign influences – Thai, Japanese, others – began to seep into French cooking, leading to *la cuisine des tendances*, which involved combinations of flavours that struck Loiseau as bizarre. He tried to accommodate his style to this new stuff from abroad, but he couldn't do it to his own satisfaction (or to that of the Michelin inspectors, who docked him a star). Despairing, he shot himself.

~~~~~

For best results, wine buyers should avoid French wine shops.

With few exceptions, vintners in France order mainly if not exclusively from local or regional vineyards, which means that in a wine-growing area you've no chance of finding a specific wine unless it happens to be local – in which case you can buy it direct from the vineyard yourself. In fact, whether you're a visitor or a resident, you should always try to buy your wine from the vineyard, where you not only have a chance to taste everything first but where, if you're going to be in the area for any length of time, you can buy *en vrac* (in bulk). It's an excellent way of picking up a lot of good wine extremely cheaply.

~~~~~

The French take their obsession with food to the grave.

Where we speak of the dead 'pushing up daisies', the French say that they *mangent les pissenlits par la racine* ('eat dandelions by the root').

~~~~~

In a country famed for its dairy products, it's difficult to find fresh milk or cream.

Despite the vast array of cheeses, butters, yoghurts and creams available, until recently it was virtually impossible to get fresh milk or fresh cream in France outside the major supermarkets. And even there you were lucky to find both. Things are beginning to improve, but searching for fresh milk or cream can still resemble a treasure hunt if you don't know where to look. Why this should be so remains a mystery – like why no one ever thought of introducing the French to the idea of self-raising flour.

~~~~~

The bread wars are being lost.

T.S. Eliot once said: "The first condition of understanding a country is to smell it." By that test, France is immediately understandable, for the incomparable, seductive aroma of freshly baked bread still wafts down the streets of every French town at all times of the day and night. Upwards of 4 million tons of bread will be sold in France this year, 75 per cent of which will come from *boulangeries*. And thanks to generous government subsidies the bread will be easily affordable. (Marie Antoinette did not die in vain.) Moreover, it will not be adulterated, as only bakers who make their own dough are allowed to call their shops *boulangeries*. So what's the problem?

The problem is that increasing prosperity and a better all-round diet have reduced dependence on bread as the most important national staple. A century ago the average French person consumed 219kg of bread per year; now the figure is below 90kg (and a mere 36 in Paris). As a result, the number of small bakers has almost halved, down to 30,000, since 1960. With the price of bread regulated, the only way that most bakers can make a decent profit is by saving on the ingredients, which means using chemicals, additives, and frozen dough. This inevitably lowers the quality, which in turn lowers the demand. The downward spiral continues.

One hopeful spin-off of this depressing cycle is the rise of the 'boutique' bakery, in which the *boulanger* bakes his bread *à l'ancienne* in a wood-fired iron oven, usually using plane and poplar logs, from dough mixed by hand and churned in a vat with nothing but hot water. I know a couple of *boulangers* who have gone back to this traditional method of making bread; while the technique may be dying out, their success with it would suggest that the taste for good bread is still very much alive.

~~~~~

The forest is a kitchen garden, if you know where to look.

At certain times throughout the year the people of south-west France carry out one of the few peacetime operations requiring precise reconnaissance information, clandestine planning and utter secrecy. The telltale signs of this operation are few: the low growl of a car's engine quietly leaving a village under cover of darkness, the sudden flash of a torch in the woods, a distant murmur of voices across the river, silhouettes at dawn fading into houses, slivers of light escaping from behind closed shutters . . . If the exercise has been successful, there will now be at least one kitchen table somewhere piled high with a splendid hoard of mushrooms recently liberated from the forest.

Although 70 per cent of the mushrooms in France come from the area around Saumur in the Loire valley, where they're cultivated *en masse*, real connoisseurs go in search of the more than 50 edible varieties that grow wild in the south-west. Among the seasonal delicacies are the *morels* and St George's mushrooms in the spring, the *girolles* and *chanterelles* in the summer, and the *cèpes* and *trompettes de la mort* in the autumn. These are sought out, and the location of their discovery guarded, with a zeal that borders on the pathological. Cars have had their tyres slashed simply for being parked a little too close to someone's secret mushroom patch. Only the ancient Egyptians and Romans, who forbade their slaves even to take part in the preparation of mushrooms, had a similar passion for the precious fungi.

One final word of caution: mushroom-hunting isn't for amateurs. If you happen to come upon some growing wild, don't assume that you've struck it rich. Take them straight to any nearby chemist, who will be able to tell you immediately which ones are edible.

~~~~~

Don't feed the pigeons; let them feed you.

Of all the game birds – which in France means practically anything with wings – there's none tastier than the young pigeon or squab, the *pigeonneau*. Although it's especially prized in the south-west, it has long been a favourite among gastronomes across France. Indeed, before the Revolution, squabs were so highly valued at court that one needed special permission from the king to have a *pigeonnier* or dovecote. Thus did the humble *pigeonnier* become a much-coveted status symbol in the 18th century.

~~~~~

Meals are getting faster, but the French aren't getting fatter.

Half of the French now spend less than 20 minutes preparing a meal, and half prefer easy-cook rice to real rice. Half eat dinner while watching television.

But a supermarket soft drink is only half the size it is in America, while a *croissant* in Paris weighs half as much as one in Pittsburgh. And half as many French as Britons are classified as obese.

~~~~~

There are at least two good reasons why French chocolate is celestial.

To begin with, *chocolatiers* in France have to undergo rigorous training. They know their stuff. In fact, the top *chocolatiers* have trained almost as long as lawyers, all in order to provide a level of pleasure that lawyers can only give by dying an agonising death. Secondly, French chocolate can have up to 86 per cent cocoa – now that's real chocolate – as contrasted with those insipid lumps of sucrose in Britain and the US that are allowed to call themselves 'chocolates' despite containing only 2 per cent cocoa.

For the experience that comes closest to going to heaven without dying first, you should go to the seaside town of Bayonne, just up the coast from Biarritz. This has to be the chocolate capital of France. In 1870 it had 130 *chocolatiers*, more than all of Switzerland. It has fewer now, but it still has its *Journées du Chocolat* in May, when the streets are adorned with elaborate statues – all in chocolate, of course.

8.

SOME SURPRISING THINGS ABOUT

FRENCH
EATING HABITS

Despite the combination of forces working to undermine traditional French eating habits, the meal remains at the heart of French family life for the overwhelming majority. The food may be faster and junkier than in the past, but the dining table nevertheless remains the centrepiece of the French home. By pitiful contrast, only half of all households in Britain even have a dining table.

~~~~~

Lunch is the principal meal of the day.

The lunch hour, which of course lasts two hours, is the pivot on which the French day turns, especially in the countryside. Even schoolchildren get two hours off for a three-course meal. And there is evidence of burglars having paused in the middle of a break-in to sit down and enjoy lunch.

~~~~~

Nor are the wider culinary implications of lunch overlooked by schools.

Lunch menus for the week are posted on school notice boards so that parents can avoid duplicating the meals at home.

~~~~~

The whole of the time reserved for lunch isn't necessarily spent over food.

The number of French men and women who return to the office after lunch wearing different clothes than they had on in the morning suggests that a significant part of some lunchtimes is spent in other 'recreational' pursuits.

~~~~~

Although lunch is the main meal, it alone may not be enough to discharge one's gastronomic obligations for the day.

As Montesquieu said, "Lunch kills half of Paris, dinner the other half." He was thinking of dinner parties in particular, where a life-threatening degree of *gourmandise* is often expected. Indeed, if you suspect that you may not have an appetite equal to the task, it's best to concoct an excuse, or invent a medical condition, beforehand to avoid insulting your hosts.

~~~~~

An invitation to dinner in a French home is not at all uncommon.

As a matter of fact, unless you're remarkably uncongenial or poorly house-trained, you're in greater danger of being overfed than overlooked.

~~~~~

There are basically three types of invitation.

Firstly, there's the invitation to *apéros*, or aperitifs. This kind of gathering typically starts at around 6 in the evening and lasts till 7.30, seldom later. If it's still going strong after an hour and a half, you should leave regardless: it will be assumed that you've another engagement that courtesy requires you to attend, and there's a good chance that your departure will trigger an exodus for which your hosts will be profoundly grateful.

Secondly, there's the *dînatoire*, which is somewhere between *apéros* and dinner. It can begin any time from 6 onwards and usually includes a buffet or some equally informal way of serving food. Being more or less unstructured, it can be open-ended. The one sure thing is that you won't need to eat afterwards.

Finally, there's the dinner party. Here the level of formality will depend on the formality of the invitation. If it's a casual invitation, it will be a casual occasion. If it's a written invitation, it will be more formal. If it includes the word *smoking*, black tie and evening dress are called for, although you won't be expected to smoke.

~~~~~

Don't expect a drink to be waiting for you when you arrive.

French hosts commonly wait for all their guests to arrive before serving drinks, even if they're an hour or more late, so pre-adjust your level of thirst to take into account the expected punctuality level of others.

~~~~~

Don't always expect to be served spirits before dinner.

In many cases you will be offered wine (from the host's cellar, not from the supermarket's shelves) or Champagne. In other cases, as the French appreciate good whisky, you may be offered a glass of single malt. *Kir* is also a popular aperitif. Named after a priest in Dijon who was a wartime Resistance hero, it's a mixture of *cassis* (blackcurrant liqueur) and white wine. When mixed with Champagne it's a *kir royal*.

At more robust gatherings, particularly in the south of France, you may be offered a *pastis*, a strong, aniseed-flavoured drink like *ouzo* or *raki*, which is diluted with water. It should be drunk with care.

~~~~~

The French have a deep abhorrence of drunkenness.

It's never, under any circumstances, acceptable or even excusable to get drunk. Nor is this simply a matter of decorum. Tedious and distasteful it may be, but more importantly it's insulting. It betrays a lack of respect for others that is only matched by the lack of respect for yourself. In a word, don't.

~~~~~

Gifts are always welcome – up to a point.

As I've already mentioned, you can seldom go wrong in bringing a gift of Champagne or chocolate or roses. A good single-malt scotch also goes down well in most instances. Best of all is the book or DVD or unusual plant that you know will appeal specially to your hosts. Whatever you decide, it's worth giving it some thought; they will, afterwards.

~~~~~

The French don't go to the loo.

For reasons that remain obscure, the French find it desirable - and, what's more, possible – to avoid going to the loo during the course of an entire evening. For those not blessed with a bladder the size of Luxembourg, this leaves two face-saving options: either go native and leave your mark *en route* where it will disorientate curious animals, or take advantage of the population shifts while people are still arriving by slipping away to the loo for a preemptive strike. And always close the door behind you when you re-emerge.

~~~~~

Bread is for breaking.

It isn't for cutting, and not for putting on your plate. The bread goes on the table beside your plate, or on the bread plate if one is provided. Buttering of bread is allowed if there's butter on the table, but it's viewed as an unfortunate thing to do to good bread.

~~~~~

The main course should be eaten hot.

Out of misplaced courtesy, guests unfamiliar with French dinner parties often wait until everyone has been served before starting on the main course. This can be unintentionally insulting to your host or hostess, who has prepared the food to be eaten when it's served, not after it has been lying around getting cold.

~~~~~

Always take less food than you intend to eat.

You will please the cook enormously by asking for seconds, but you will not be forgiven if you leave something uneaten.

~~~~~

It isn't a compliment to ask for the recipe.

For a start, it assumes that the dish you liked came from a cookery book rather than from the cook's own imagination and expertise.

Not only that but, given the amount of personal care and attention that goes into a dish, it's like asking someone if he would mind if you forged his signature a few times.

~~~~~

Never pour the wine yourself.

That's the host's job. There could be any number of reasons why your glass is not being refilled at the rate you might wish, but none of them justifies taking matters into your own hands.

~~~~~

Be careful how you cut the cheese.

This, too, is a job best left to your host. But if you're encouraged to help yourself, make sure you never slice the point off a triangular wedge of soft cheese; always cut off a slice from along the side of the wedge.

~~~~~

As in poker, keep your hands visible at the table.

This rather arcane custom is thought to have originated at a time when hands that were out of sight were assumed to be up to no good – perhaps exploring a lap other than one's own.

~~~~~

Cutlery is part of the conversation.

To say 'I've finished', place your knife and fork side by side pointing upwards from four o'clock to ten.

There's only one secret to giving a successful dinner party in France.

It's this: whatever goes wrong, make a joke out of it. Actually, that's the secret of a successful dinner party anywhere. Laughter is the perfect *digestif*. Panic, on the other hand, can spoil the taste of anything – and it stays in the memory longer. For that reason I remember well the first dinner party I attended after moving here. The hosts were afflicted with the sort of barely-concealed anxiety that guarantees disaster. Sure enough, it was only a matter of minutes before someone's drink had been knocked over and smoke was billowing out from under the kitchen door. I don't remember whose drink hit the floor, or even what was accidentally incinerated, but the Laurel-and-Hardyesque sideshow of accusations and recriminations was unforgettable. Remember, then: whatever happens, it will make a funny story at your next dinner party, so you might as well start laughing now.

If only the Prince de Condé's chef had had the benefit of this insight in 1671 when he was in charge of preparing a dinner that the prince was giving in honour of Louis XIV. Panic-stricken when the seafood didn't arrive in time, the chef took out his sword and killed himself. It's said to have ruined the king's evening.

9.

SOME SURPRISING THINGS ABOUT

FRENCH
RESTAURANTS

If there's anything more important to the French than their friendships, it's their restaurants. This may sound a little far-fetched, but according to one study the notion has more than a grain of truth to it. Researchers asked people from 40 countries to imagine that they were restaurant critics whose closest friend had sunk his life savings into a new restaurant. But when they went there, as critics, they found that the food was awful. The problem: how should they review the restaurant? Should they, in other words, go easy on it out of regard for their friendship?

Britons were about evenly divided, whereas a majority of Americans thought they should tell the truth. But no fewer than four out of five of the French insisted that they would criticise the restaurant as harshly as it deserved.

~~~~~

We have the Revolution to thank for the institution of great French restaurants.

With the disappearance of the old aristocracy, a lot of first-class chefs suddenly became unemployed. So they put themselves to work by founding the first restaurants in Paris.

~~~~~

A fragile temperament is necessary to become a top French chef.

It may not be strictly necessary, but it helps. When a young friend of Dana Facaros, co-author of the excellent Cadogan guide to France, completed his degree course in cookery, his final exam consisted of preparing a meal from the ingredients provided by the examiners. On being given a whole, unplucked chicken for the main course, he threw a tantrum at being expected to pluck his own chicken. He was awarded two extra points for having the right attitude.

~~~~~

The first celebrity chef was French.

The man credited with being the founder of classic French *haute cuisine* in the early 19th century, Antonin Carême was also the first chef to publish his own cookery books.

~~~~~

In Paris, it's worth asking if the chef is from the Aveyron.

Even if he isn't, there's a good chance that the proprietor, or the *sous-chef*, or the waiter, or the sommelier is, such is the extent to which the Aveyronnais dominate the Parisian restaurant scene. I have on several occasions enjoyed special treatment in the capital's restaurants and hotels by the simple expedient of inventing a distant relative in the Aveyron.

~~~~~

The Gault-Millau guide is superior to the Michelin.

The Gault-Millau is more reliable because it has a more complex and helpful system of rating restaurants, whereas the Michelin is more likely to be influenced by big reputations (which it probably helped to create in the first place). Indeed, in early 2005 Michelin was forced to pulp 50,000 copies of its *Red Guide* to the Benelux countries when it was caught having awarded high marks to a restaurant that was still a building site at the time it was supposedly inspected.

The menu in French restaurants isn't a menu.

It's a set meal, with a choice for each course, at a set price. *La carte* is the menu. And on it the *entrées* are starters, the entry into the meal, and not the main dishes, which are *plats*.

~~~~~

A well done steak isn't well done.

Should you want a steak for your main course, very rare (blood-red) is *bleu*, rare is *saignant*, and medium is *à point*. If you like it well done, why did you leave home?

And if you don't know what *steak tartare* is, ask before ordering it.

~~~~~

Never bring your own wine to a restaurant, however special the wine or the occasion.

The reasons should be obvious. If not, trust me.

~~~~~

In a good restaurant, don't expect to find salt and pepper on the table.

As a rule, the better the restaurant, the less likely you are to find that the chef is willing to risk letting you interfere with his food without at least tasting it first. If after tasting it you think that it's inadequately seasoned, and aren't worried by the thought of making a mortal enemy in the kitchen, by all means ask for salt and pepper.

French restaurants frequently have unisex loos.

There will usually be a *cabinet* for men and one for women, in the same room, flanking a wash basin and mirror which is used by both. Others have less private arrangements. Get used to it.

~~~~~

If the waiter is slow in bringing your bill, it isn't because he's ignoring you.

On the contrary, he's being thoughtful and not rushing you. An essential part of any French meal is the conversation that follows it, possibly accompanied by liqueurs or brandy or extra coffee, and no waiter would be so foolish as to intrude on this (with the exception of a waiter in a café who is going off duty and needs to cash out, but he will usually apologise for the interruption).

~~~~~

The tip is included.

All restaurant bills, by the way, come with *service compris*: the tip is included. You are of course free to add to it as a gesture of thanks for particularly friendly or attentive service.

~~~~~

There aren't so many cafés in France.

That's because they've gone out of business. A century ago there were more than 500,000 cafés and bars in France; today there are fewer than 50,000, and they're closing at the rate of 3,000 a year – half of them in Paris. These statistics are particularly melancholy insofar as they affect the older cafés – those "parliaments of the people", as Balzac called them – where the French traditionally went to talk, argue, read, write, meditate, make notes, hold meetings, wink at the girls, or just linger over coffee in the sun.

And what has replaced them? 'English' and 'Irish' pubs and fast-food outlets, including 1,200 *'hamburgeries'*. Of these almost half are McDonald's, or *McDos*. It's little wonder that José Bové, the bucolic scourge of McDonald's, has become something of a cult hero.

~~~~~

Children and dogs are welcome in most restaurants.

Dogs may not be greeted with much enthusiasm, but they will be cheerfully tolerated if they're well behaved. Children, on the other hand, are always welcome because they're always well behaved. French children can sit still for hours, eating with perfect manners, joining in the conversation. The contrast with the behaviour of American children (and the noisier ones among the British) is so striking that French parents assume, charitably, that the children must be autistic or retarded.

~~~~~

Away from the cities, eating well can be a hit-or-miss proposition.

There are, thankfully, still thousands of superb restaurants all over France where the regional specialities, in particular, offer a glorious dining experience. And at the other end of the scale the *routiers* still provide splendid five-course meals with wine for only a few euros. The *routiers* may not be in the guidebooks, but they can be graded by their own non-Michelin system: instead of counting stars, you count the number of HGVs parked outside at lunchtime.

In between the country restaurants and *routiers* are the *auberges* and *tables d'hôte*. The food served in these places is usually reliable, and sometimes exceptional, because the diners are often also staying there as paying guests.

The real disappointment is what has happened to the provincial bistros. These used to be jolly family affairs, with *Maman* and *Papa* and all the kids and cousins and in-laws pitching in to produce hearty meals at bargain prices. But gradually the meals have become less hearty and less of a bargain, as one by one the bistros have fallen victim to a classic economic squeeze. The younger members of the family drifted off to university or to the cities, others married and moved away, the parents grew too old or too tired to cope on their own, the bureaucracy made it prohibitively expensive to hire new staff, which led to corners being cut and compromises made, until the old bistro was only a memory.

Simon Davis, the travel editor of the London *Evening Standard*, has a house in Normandy and he says that he is constantly "amazed by how ghastly the food is in the majority of provincial French bistros. We have reached a point where much of the food offered in a British pub is superior to that available in a French bistro." Sadly true.

~~~~~

Café au lait is for dunking.

The standard cup of coffee in France – *un café* – is made in an espresso machine and served black in a *demi-tasse*. A large one is a *café noir double*. If you want an extra strong coffee, *un café serré* has only half the usual amount of hot water; if you want it weak, *un café allongé* has double the usual hot water. If you see others being served black coffee in large cups and want to be sure of receiving a small, strong one, ask for *un express*. A coffee with steamed milk is *un café crème*, or simply *un crème*; a large one is *un grand crème*. A *café au lait* is only ever served at breakfast – in a bowl, so that you can dip your croissant in it.

~~~~~

In France, you can drink all day . . . and all night.

As there are no licensing hours in France, you can order alcoholic drinks at any time of the day or night, but it's assumed (and fondly hoped, for your sake) that your one for the road will be coffee.

10.

SOME SURPRISING THINGS ABOUT

FRENCH SHOPS

A few years ago, needing to fly to Izmir in Turkey, I went into a Toulouse travel agent to see what flights were available. With one exception – a direct flight from Nantes, 600km away – all the flights that were feasible involved going to Paris and taking Air France from there via Istanbul or going to either Frankfurt or Zurich and waiting for hours to join a Lufthansa flight. As I'm allergic both to Air France and to waiting, I decided to drive to Nantes and fly from there. Having made my decision, I then had to wait to see another lady who made the actual reservations. After a long conversation involving a third person about whether my credit card automatically had travel insurance, the reservations were made.

Sort of.

I was told that confirmation would arrive in the post during the week before I was due to fly. No other information was available, such as check-in time or exact time of departure. Finally, two days before I was due to leave, all the information, but no tickets, arrived.

Fast forward to Nantes. At the airport I was told that I couldn't check in without my tickets. Finally, after an hour or so queuing, I got the tickets that entitled me to stand in another queue to check in. Now at last clutching all the stuff that could have been issued weeks earlier, I went into the departure lounge, where the only functioning dispenser of refreshments was a soft drinks machine. By the time I got to Izmir I'd forgotten why I was there.

What this sad little parable illustrates is the first principle of making a purchase in France: if there's an obvious, straightforward, commonsense way of conducting a transaction, it will never be used so long as there's an interminable, inexplicable, Byzantine procedure available that keeps the maximum number of people in employment.

Not all bargains come gift-wrapped in red tape.

Have a poke round the *brocantes* (shops selling second-hand items), *marchés aux puces* (flea markets), *vides greniers* (attic sales), and of course the weekly town markets. These are for real shoppers.

~~~~~

The department store was invented in France.

The world's first department store was *Au Bon Marché*, which opened in 1852. Carrefour opened the first hypermarket in 1963. It now has 600 stores throughout France, and accounts for 50 per cent of all French food sales. Only Wal-Mart is bigger worldwide.

~~~~~

Don't try to replace items bought in French supermarkets.

Unless you want to find out how many people can be gainfully employed in not being helpful. Likewise, if you return faulty electronic equipment, they will insist on sending it for repair – which can take weeks or months – rather than simply exchanging it.

~~~~~

Tobacconists have a monopoly on the sale of tobacco.

This monopoly was originally granted by Napoleon as a form of compensation to the thousands of French widows created by the imperial adventures of the *Grande Armée*. The right was then passed down from one generation to the next. In addition to tobacco products, *tabacs* sell postage stamps, lottery tickets, *télécartes* for use in public telephones, prepaid recharging for mobile phones, stationery, post cards, gifts, souvenirs, photo supplies, and various government stamps.

Tabacs often double as a newsagent's or bar and are instantly identifiable by their vertical orange signs. The sign represents a carrot, and dates from the time when carrots were put in with tobacco to keep it moist.

~~~~~

Shops are allowed to hold sales only at specified times.

Sales must be held from mid-January to mid-February and from mid-June to mid-July. The government sets the exact dates, and any exceptions must be cleared in advance with the police, who are responsible for enforcing the laws regarding sales. To hold a sale outside the authorised times is a criminal offence punishable by fines or imprisonment. All sales, too, must be real sales – prices cannot be marked up beforehand in order to be marked down during a sale.

These sale laws originated with the medieval guilds, which set standards for quality and pricing and were responsible for protecting local tradesmen against competition from other towns.

~~~~~

Shop floors are about giving employment, not service.

The French have no concept of service as we understand it. As selling isn't a respected profession in France, salespeople tend to see customers as strangers who look down on them. Therefore they have no reason to care whether the customers are satisfied or not.

The trick is to give them a reason to care. Some find that determined friendliness works; others say that abject helplessness, perhaps with a dash of desperation, will win them over. Everyone agrees that any display of anger or exasperation is futile. If they had any fear of you, or fear of being sacked, they wouldn't have antagonised you in the first place.

Nor would the government feel it necessary to appeal to them every year to try to be nice to tourists.

~~~~~

Take baskets and a euro with you to supermarkets.

As you will have to bag your purchases anyway, you might as well organise it straight into your own baskets and cool bags. The euro is for the shopping trolley, and is automatically refunded when you take the trolley back to its station.

~~~~~

Be prepared to pay in advance for dry cleaning.

Dry cleaning (*pressing*) is expensive in France, and usually you will be expected to pay in advance. The worst (and dearest) dry cleaners are those in the malls attached to supermarkets.

~~~~~

Never pay for anything at your front door.

Door-to-door salespeople aren't allowed to take money in France. They can only take orders.

Yes, you can touch the bananas.

. . . and every other fruit or vegetable. Somehow the idea has got round that stallholders in French markets object to having their produce handled or sniffed. This is nonsense. In some cases they will want to help do the selecting for you, but they will be just as fussy – only faster.

~~~~~

Shops are closed on Sundays . . . and Mondays.

Not all shops are closed, of course, and not everywhere. But in general you should not expect shops or museums or good restaurants to be open on Mondays, although you will always find a bakery or a pharmacy open somewhere nearby.

~~~~~

Anything will be gift-wrapped free of charge.

Shopkeepers are always happy to wrap any item *pour offrir* (bought as a gift), and most are adept at creating imaginatively wrapped packages of great charm.

~~~~~

Credit cards aren't accepted everywhere.

Most French shoppers pay by cash or cheque. While it's becoming more common to see people using bank cards, or *cartes bleues*, these are debit cards and can only be used with their PIN. The French find the very idea of credit cards, or for that matter overdrafts, puzzling. So even though credit cards are widely accepted now, in some out-of-the-way places it may be necessary to explain that you're using old-fashioned plastic requiring a signature.

~~~~~

The regular customer is king.

If you become a regular, you will cease to be a stranger in at least one corner of a land that has a congenital suspicion of strangers, whether foreign or home-grown. Moreover, your repeat custom won't go unnoticed or unappreciated: the French place a premium on loyalty. Lastly, there are the obvious advantages of having a shopkeeper who knows your tastes and likely requirements.

As a side benefit, you will probably discover that the shopkeeper whom you once thought rude for ignoring you was in fact just being courteous to someone else. After all, most of his customers are shopping for conversation as well as merchandise.

~~~~~

Supermarkets are good places to buy clothes.

No kidding. Even if money is no object, you can often find attractive and stylish items in the clothes sections of the big supermarkets. It's always worth a look.

~~~~~

There are some things money cannot buy.

One of the immutable laws of travel is that in every country there's something you cannot get which is available in every other country in the known world. In France, it's the small plain white notepad.

You might want to make a note of this, while you can.

~~~~~

Don't hesitate to stock up on hard-to-find items.

This is the only sure way of outwitting the gremlins who roam French supermarket aisles at night making things disappear from the shelves, often for months at a time. Don't assume they will reappear just because there may be a demand for them. Buy them while you can. The worst that can happen is that you end up with a five-years supply of deodorant and peanut butter.

~~~~~

What British expatriates in France miss most is . . . Waitrose.

According to a recent survey, at least. Admittedly, the survey was neither wide-ranging nor scientific, having been conducted by me in a shamelessly haphazard manner. Nonetheless, one couldn't help being struck by the fact that, up there with the English language and sense of humour, family and friends, everyone mentioned Waitrose. Not Sainsbury, not Tesco, certainly not Safeway. Waitrose. Whatever else this may mean, it means there's a sociological monograph crying out to be written.

11.

SOME SURPRISING THINGS ABOUT

FRENCH
ATTITUDES TO MONEY

The announcement by the Banque de France of the date when the euro would permanently replace the franc detonated one of the great consumer stampedes of modern times. At one stroke, millions of bank notes were liberated from inside mattresses, behind walls, under floorboards, as people rushed to convert their paper stashes into things. Overnight, farmers were driving BMWs as well as tractors, their wives were wearing jewellery the size of Christmas decorations, and holiday homes began spreading like a rash across the landscape.

At the same time as all this cash escaped from captivity, so too did one of the most closely guarded secrets of the French: one reason the French don't like talking about money is that it might not be in their interest for outsiders to start counting it.

~~~~~

There are good reasons for the French distaste for the subject of money.

To begin with, the French do genuinely find the subject vulgar and inconsequential in the overall scheme of things. After all, you cannot have a decent conversation with it, you cannot make love to it, you cannot hang it on the wall or listen to it, you cannot read it or watch it in performance, you cannot eat it or drink it, you cannot wear it, you cannot even heat the room, tile the roof or plant the garden with it.

How can money possibly be interesting in itself when its sole function is to make other things interesting? The simple answer, which the French have worked out, is that it isn't in the least interesting except insofar as it provides access to people, places and things of interest. Which alone obliges them to consider ways of handling it when they have it.

Not all French banks are French.

If you're planning to spend any serious amount of time in France, or are contemplating buying property in France, you should have a French bank account. As there are only a relative handful of French banks, with no real competition between them, it doesn't much matter which one you choose. They all have basically the same services, including online banking.

Expatriates, however, might be more comfortable banking with Barclays, which now has over 100 branches in France. Citibank also has several branches, while the Banque Transatlantique has been established specifically with the expatriate in mind.

~~~~~

Cheques are used almost as frequently as cash.

But you have to be careful how you use them. There are no cheque guarantee cards in France: what in effect guarantees them are the severe penalties if you bounce one. Should you be careless enough to write a cheque without the funds to cover it, and the situation isn't put right immediately, you will be blacklisted by the Banque de France, cutting off your access to future credit within the French banking system.

~~~~~

You cannot change your mind about a cheque you've written.

Once you've paid for something by cheque, you cannot unilaterally decide that the payment was in error. You can stop payment on cheques only if your chequebook has been lost or stolen.

It's illegal to be overdrawn in France without prior authorisation.

Unlike British banks, which take a fairly relaxed attitude to overdrafts, merely raising the ceiling on them or increasing the fees payable on them whenever you wander over their limit, perhaps sending you a gentlemanly reminder if you don't seem to be paying attention, French banks take a very dim view of people who don't keep their spending strictly within their means.

~~~~~

Regular bills should be paid by direct debit.

If you own property in France, whether you live there or simply visit from time to time, it's a good idea to have all your regular bills – electricity, telephone, water, house and car insurance, local taxes – paid by direct debit, or *prélèvement*. Annual charges such as taxes and insurance can also be paid monthly, and charges subject to seasonal fluctuations, such as heating oil, can be averaged out and spread over the year.

~~~~~

Safeguard your RIBs.

The *relevé d'identité bancaire*, or *RIB*, is a slip of paper that comes with your chequebook and serves many essential purposes. In fact, it's required in so many different situations that you should ask the bank for extra copies or make photocopies yourself. The *RIB* has all your bank details on it and will be required whenever you're setting up direct debits or standing orders, or paying certain official fees, or transferring money, and in various other circumstances where financial identification is needed.

Safeguard your PINs.

Sensibly, the French long ago abandoned the requirement for a signature whenever a bank card is used in favour of a four-digit code. Not only is it much more secure, but it's much more convenient for everyone involved, except perhaps for people who have a problem remembering four numbers in a row – and they already have bigger problems than that to worry about.

~~~~~

Bank card charges aren't debited until the end of the month.

This means that you should keep an eye on the sums you charge to the card, because they won't appear on the balance statements issued by cash machines. But they will show up all at once on the last working day of the month.

~~~~~

It's wise to carry more than one card.

French bank cards have ludicrously low limits on cash withdrawals, so if you're going to need money from a cash machine, you should use a card more sympathetic to your immediate needs.

~~~~~

There's a risk in paying people in cash.

Many non-professional people – handymen, cleaning ladies, gardeners – will expect to be paid in cash, on the side, *au noir*. This has two obvious advantages: it means you get a favourable deal, as you don't have to pay VAT, while it saves your employee having to pay income tax or social security contributions on the invisible earnings.

But it does carry significant disadvantages. For example, if either of you has made any enemies, knowingly or otherwise, or if the person working for you has a jealous rival who resents his or her good fortune, you could be denounced to the tax authorities, in which case you could both be heavily fined, or worse. It should be said that the chances of being thus reported are vanishingly small – I've never heard of such a case – as are the chances of anyone being able to prove that moonlit readies changed hands. Still, the possibility exists, which, combined with the inexhaustible malevolence of revenue ferrets, is worth taking into account.

The second risk is at once more of a threat and more likely to have serious consequences. It's the risk of injury to someone you've employed 'on the black', with the consequent liability for damages if you're successfully sued.

~~~~~

French tradesmen are used to late payment.

This is a fact, not an incitement to ignore bills. French tradesmen, in particular the busier ones, frequently wait weeks or even months before sending a bill. Indeed, I know of instances where people are still waiting to receive bills for work completed years ago. Likewise, few people lunge for their chequebook every time a bill arrives. This reflects the personal circumstances of neither, but rather the French desire not to appear to place more importance on money than it deserves.

My own feeling is that a little thoughtfulness is called for here. For example, if you've had work done which required someone to buy parts or hire equipment to do the job, it's unfair to leave him out of pocket when the job is completed. If, on the other hand, the job was done with an heroic lack of urgency, payment according to the same schedule would seem to be justified.

12.

SOME SURPRISING THINGS ABOUT

FRENCH
BUREAUCRACY

A nn Wroe, the distinguished author of *A Fool and His Money*, that compelling story of life in medieval France, recalls the time she wandered across a deserted French square on a Sunday morning: "I was made by a policeman to go back and cross it at the designated place." Why? "Bureaucracy, for the love of it."

She was fortunate not to have had to produce her papers as well.

~~~~~

French fonctionnaires don't believe you exist unless you have the papiers to prove it.

It's the civil servant's ultimate perversion of the Cartesian *Cogito ergo sum*. Perhaps the most celebrated example of the primacy of one's existence on paper came in the 1960s when young Eric Peugeot, son of the automobile tycoon, was kidnapped. After a nationwide search, the police received a tip-off that led to his rescue. When his mother arrived at the police station to be tearfully reunited with her son, she told the *gendarme* at the door, somewhat superfluously: "I am Madame Peugeot." Stone-faced, the *gendarme* replied: "Your papers, Madame."

~~~~~

The less important an official, the more officious he's likely to be.

Some years ago, a well known French anthropologist returned from working among the Mayan ruins in South America in order to have a baby. However, when she tried to register the baby's name as Maya, the local town registrar refused to allow it. He had never heard of such a name. In the end she had to drive to a city where the registry officers were happy to let her name her baby as she wished.

A quarter of the entire French workforce consists of bureaucrats.

That's twice as many as in Germany and is a proportion matched only in Scandinavia. In raw numbers, it adds up to 6 million people working for the state.

~~~~~

Your creative offspring are subject to state scrutiny as well.

When an American couple took up residence near Cahors some years ago, the government wanted proof that they were self-employed. Both authors, they were asked to send copies of some of their books to Paris. The books were returned with an official certificate confirming the couple's status as intellectuals.

In the 19th century, paintings had to be registered with the government before they could be offered for sale. Disappointingly, there's no record of anyone painting a 'Still Life with Official Forms' as a silent comment on this regulation.

~~~~~

Form-filling is a national pastime.

Whatever you want to do, you can safely assume that at some stage it will involve seemingly endless form-filling. Everything requires paperwork. What makes it seem endless is the French obsession with classification. Nothing arouses so much horror in the bureaucratic breast as a space left blank on a form.

My first experience of this came when I went to get insurance for my French car. After I'd answered a number of questions to the agent's apparent satisfaction, we came to the question of my occupation.

"Writer," I said. Carefully, then with growing anxiety, he went repeatedly through the list of recognised occupations. The list didn't include 'Writer'. Utter consternation. Finally, rather than leave the space blank, he decided to put down whatever category seemed a safe bet. After several surreptitious glances across the desk at me while pretending to be deep in thought, he wrote: *Retraité non-agricole*. Although the literal translation – 'non-agricultural pensioner' – was relatively inoffensive, I took it as code for 'face re-touched by over-indulgence, hands untouched by labour'. I did my best not to look aggrieved.

~~~~~

Never throw anything away.

Keep every scrap of paper that wafts into sight, and let no paper out of your sight without keeping a copy; this includes estimates, bills, receipts, delivery notes and all correspondence. Any document relating to a financial transaction should be kept: salary statements, for instance, must by law be kept for life. Likewise, from your point of view it's always advisable to keep a written record of important matters. Something in writing always carries more weight; a registered letter, in fact, constitutes binding legal proof of the transmission of information.

Whenever furnishing a French residence, therefore, start with a photocopier and a fax machine – and a big pile of blank paper. It won't remain blank for long.

~~~~~

Corsica is the true cradle of bureaucracy.

Unknown even to many French themselves, Corsicans have long been the backbone of the mainland civil service (not to mention the

Foreign Legion, the security forces, and the Marseille underworld). But it makes sense when you think about it. If someone is needed to fill an underpaid, under-rated job that requires an uncanny knack for knowing where to look for evidence of misconduct, and a remarkably thick skin when dealing with the public – and preferably someone who enjoys terrorising large numbers of people without regard for the widespread loathing this engenders – then where better to recruit than Corsica? It is, after all, an island where less than 10 per cent of the population pays any income tax although car ownership is above the national average.

~~~~~

France's biggest annual sporting contest is Tax Dodgers v. Tax Collectors.

This is how it's played.

1. The Dodgers are given a head start. Because France, unlike other industrialised nations, doesn't tax income at source, the Dodgers start out with money in their pockets that elsewhere would have been automatically deducted from their wages.

2. The Dodgers then head for the woods, across a deadly minefield of indirect taxes, with the Collectors in distant pursuit.

3. Once they're out of sight of their pursuers, the Dodgers look for places to hide the money that survived the indirect taxation.

4. Eventually the Collectors catch up with them and start taking prisoners. At this stage about half of the Dodgers escape.

5. After a lengthy interrogation of the other half, the location of a lot of the hidden money is discovered, and everyone, guilty or not, gets fined on principle.

6. Both sides declare victory, because a lot of money has been recovered, and a lot has gone unrecovered.

Of course the real winners are the sponsors of the Tax Collectors, the bureaucracy, because they get paid just for fielding a team, and the real losers are the spectators who pay their taxes and thus are forced to subsidise both teams.

~~~~~

France has become a leading exporter of refugees from bureaucracy.

The unthinkable is happening: French restaurateurs are at the forefront of an exodus from the tyranny of the bureaucrats. Faced with the obstacle course of red tape anyone must surmount to start a business in France, restaurateurs are increasingly going abroad, often overseas, to establish new restaurants.

And there are now 300,000 French living in the UK, the largest French expatriate colony in Europe. They overwhelmingly cite freedom from bureaucratic regulation as their reason for moving.

13.

SOME SURPRISING THINGS ABOUT

FRENCH
HEALTHCARE

The French health service is justly renowned as the best in the world. It isn't just a matter of more good doctors, or more good hospitals, or more up-to-date medical equipment, or more swift attention to patients' needs. It's a combination of all those things, and a lot more besides.

Yes, there are more doctors: three per 1,000 of the population, compared to 1.7 per 1,000 in the UK. And they're prepared to make house calls at any time of the day or night (a third of all medical consultations are done at home!), although there are unhappy signs that this is beginning to change. For less serious cases, there are the French pharmacists, who are both qualified and authorised to give medical advice, including diagnoses and recommendations regarding the appropriate medication.

Yes, there are more hospitals, with 8.5 beds per 1,000 people, twice as many as in the UK or US. What's more, the hospitals are fully staffed and have state-of-the-art equipment. And for urgent cases there's a highly efficient system of emergency services – including the firemen, all of whom are trained paramedics – which means that everyone is within minutes of treatment and hospital care.

Yes, the medical technology is superb. But more to the point, it's comprehensively available. Even our local dentist, who spends her days peering into the black holes of farmers' mouths, has an array of equipment, including the most sophisticated 3-D imaging apparatus, that would make most British dentists drool with envy.

But what makes French healthcare so special is the way all those factors – more health professionals, more efficient delivery of services, better facilities, superior equipment – are integrated into a patient-centred system. The patient's needs always come first – including, most importantly, the need to know what's going on. Information is part of the treatment. So is the doctor's willingness to use homeopathy or other 'alternative' remedies. There's also a sympathetic understanding of the hospitalised patient's situation, in which physical discomfort may be less 'painful' than the demoralising indignities that are a consequence of helplessness. It's this approach, this ability to deal with symptoms that don't show up in measurements or lab reports, that sets the French system of healthcare apart from others.

~~~~~

Pharmacies play a crucial role in the healthcare system.

French pharmacies are fundamentally different from British chemists' or American drugstores. For one thing, they exist principally for medical reasons; most of them sell few, if any, cosmetics or beauty products. For another, they must be owned and run by trained pharmacists; their numbers are strictly controlled, and 'chain' pharmacies are illegal. (Nevertheless, whenever a pharmacy is closed, a notice must be posted in the window giving the name and address of the nearest one that's open.)

French pharmacists have considerable diagnostic expertise, and can be trusted to give sound advice. When filling prescriptions, they will usually ask if you would like them to substitute cheaper generic equivalents for branded drugs, and they're also familiar with the full range of homeopathic remedies. Above all, they're scrupulous about looking after your welfare. Once I went into a pharmacy to buy a brace to support a knee that I'd twisted. The pharmacist examined the knee carefully, and then refused to sell me a brace until I'd had the knee X-rayed. After getting it X-rayed at a nearby hospital (a procedure that took all of 45 minutes, by the way, from the moment I hobbled unannounced into the hospital), I took the pictures back to the pharmacist for examination; he then he fitted me with a brace.

Coincidentally or not, the French are a nation of hypochondriacs.

They visit the doctor more often than other Europeans, and take more prescription drugs. They insist on injections even for such routine conditions as the common cold. Over 12 per cent complain of having migraines, while everyone complains of having a dodgy liver. They're prescribed an average of 37 packets of pills each per annum (compared to nine a year in the UK).

~~~~~

Of course, the food is good in French hospitals.

In fact, the food in the state-run hospitals is better than it is in private clinics. This is because the four-course meals laid on in the hospitals are made possible by special grants, whereas the private clinics have to finance their more modest fare out of their own resources. But, as with other aspects of French healthcare, hospital meals are beginning to be affected by a decline in standards.

~~~~~

When it comes to nervous breakdowns, the French are closing in on the Americans.

They may not have caught up yet, but that could be due to the fact that the French lead the world in taking psychotropic drugs: sleeping pills, tranquillisers, anti-depressants and so on. (This may well play a hidden part in another statistic, the high number of traffic fatalities, as it's estimated that at any given time up to half of French drivers are narcoleptic.) Even so, in the last ten years there has been an 86 per cent rise in the number of psychiatric internments.

For the French, all health – good or ill – starts with the liver.

It's impossible to overstate the French obsession with the liver (*le foie*) – although this may not be so odd, considering what the average French liver has to cope with. As the American humourist Art Buchwald once observed, "A bad liver is to a Frenchman what a nervous breakdown is to an American. Everyone has one and everyone wants to talk about it."

~~~~~

France has the highest incidence of AIDS in Europe.

This is largely due to the large segment of the population from sub-Saharan Africa, and to the fact that there has been a lamentably inadequate public information campaign by the government to promote 'safe sex' and other preventative measures.

~~~~~

France is a good place to visit when you're ill.

In the distant past, Britons would regularly make the boast abroad that they had the best available health insurance: an NHS card and a return ticket. Now, alas, it's the other way round. By the end of 2005 all European Union countries will have replaced the old E111 (and its relatives, the E110, E119 and E128) with the new European Health Insurance Card (EHIC) to cover medical expenses incurred elsewhere in the EU. Foreign residents of France can already obtain the French version of the EHIC, the *Carte Européenne d'Assurance Maladie* (*CEAM*). In a country notorious for strangling people with red tape, the system for dealing with illness is surprisingly hassle-free.

You can see any doctor at any time.

If you're merely feeling under the weather, don't forget that you can pop in to see any doctor during the hours when his or her surgery is open to the public, or by appointment at other times. The fee for a consultation is only €20.

~~~~~

The French may not be renowned as animal lovers, but their vets are first-rate.

Sick pets are very well cared for in the veterinary clinics, which are equipped to an enviably high standard. If the pet lives in France, even part-time, you will be given a dossier with its full medical history and record of inoculations; you will also be sent reminders whenever any sort of treatment is due.

~~~~~

Health isn't about money.

So why is the French health service so good? Perhaps it's a mark of the overriding French concern with health in general, or perhaps health is the point where two dominant French obsessions – with sensuality and with order – intersect. The only thing one can say for certain is that it isn't a question of money. French employees pay on average a little more than 10 per cent of their earnings for all their social security benefits, including healthcare and pensions. Their American counterparts, by comparison, pay a similar amount for their health insurance alone. Yet according to the United Nations rankings, French healthcare is the best on earth. The US is ranked 37th.

14.

SOME SURPRISING THINGS ABOUT
FRENCH DRIVING

If there's one thing that definitively sets the French apart from everyone else who has ever been to France, it's their rather touching belief that they aren't among the worst drivers in the world. Their roads may be the best in Europe, yet twice as many people are killed on them annually as in Britain; indeed, some of them have claimed more victims than the average battlefield.

The French have the most stringent driving test in Europe, yet they produce drivers who manage to be incompetent and rude at the same time.

And, contrary to what one might expect, especially if one has experience of other places where driving is the inarticulate or inadequate person's way of making a statement, the women are as bad as the men.

~~~~~

Trees are to blame for many accidents.

To the neutral observer, it may look as if the trees standing by the roadside are minding their own business when French drivers, as they're frequently inclined to do, veer off the road at high speed and crash into them. But the French see it differently. They view the trees as a sinister threat to their freedom to drive like maniacs. So they cut them down. They cut them down in their millions, as if in reprisal for the road fatalities. As a result, thousands of kilometres of beautiful tree-lined roads have been stripped of their canopy of shade simply to prolong the life expectancy of bad drivers.

Tellingly, the metaphor for crashing your car is *casser du bois*, 'to break some wood'.

Even though, of course, it's the wood's fault.

Forty per cent of fatal road accidents involve drivers who have been drinking.

This is in spite of severe penalties for being over the legal limit (which happens to be much lower than in the UK). Indeed, drivers who exceed the permitted alcohol limit can be sentenced to two years in prison, or four years' community service with a €4,600 fine, even if they haven't caused a serious accident.

However draconian the penalties for drinking and driving, it's still rare to see a Frenchman forego one for the other. It's as if a Frenchman's rightful place is behind the wheel no matter what, and not in the back seat of a taxi or (God forbid!) in the passenger seat while a female companion drives.

~~~~~

Many other accidents involve prescription drugs.

As far as I'm aware, nobody knows exactly how many. But what is known is that a frightening number of people are driving around sedated on tranquillisers, and it's reasonable to infer that they drive even more dangerously when in a semi-stupor than when fully conscious.

~~~~~

Car lights are used for sending various kinds of message.

Headlights on during the day can mean that the driver recently passed through a foggy patch and hasn't got round to switching his lights off, or he may know that driving with the lights on at all times is strongly recommended by the police in most areas. Headlight flashing, on the other hand, is strongly disapproved of by the police, as it's a warning that the *gendarmes* are lying in wait by the road ahead.

Indicators are only occasionally used to herald a turn. Frequently they're used to indicate that the driver is going to move around 10cm to the left to pass a cyclist, but most often it's a last-second warning that the driver is about to overtake another car.

If there are neither cars nor cyclists ahead of a car with flashing indicators, it means that the driver has forgotten all about them.

~~~~~

Saturday nights and Sunday afternoons are the most dangerous times to be on the road.

In the former instance, it should be assumed that the driver has had at least one for the road; in the latter, the driver is probably coming home from feasting with the family, and thus has undoubtedly taken on board too much of something. Watch out especially for older men wearing a flat cap and driving a 2CV. I have no statistical proof, but I'm willing to bet that they cause more accidents, directly or indirectly, than anything else that moves.

~~~~~

Like Nature, the French abhor a vacuum.

The single most annoying, and most perilous, habit among French drivers is their practice of driving as close behind you as possible without actually hitting you. Because they do this at all speeds, your chances of being hit increase as the speed of the traffic fluctuates. 'Tailgating', as the Americans call it, is known in France as *'coller aux fesses'* – 'sticking to the buttocks' – and is another of their misdemeanours (driving within two seconds of the car in front is now illegal) that they seem blissfully unaware of committing.

~~~~~

The French overtake just for the hell of it.

There's something about the sight of a car in front of them that releases a red mist in the brains of all French drivers, creating an uncontrollable urge either to get as close as possible to the car in front or to overtake it, irrespective of oncoming traffic or the imminence of a blind bend. Indeed, these little impedimenta only seem to add to the thrill of the exercise, which reaches its climax when the overtaken driver refuses to let the overtaker back in. As Peter Mayle says, "A French driver considers it a moral defeat to give way."

What happens then? One of three things:

1. The most likely is that the overtaking driver is forced to *faire une queue de poisson* – 'do a fishtail' – by swerving and cutting in.

2. Another possibility is that the overtaker *rentre dans le décor* – 'goes into the scenery' – by driving off the road, where he will probably make contact with a blameworthy tree.

3. The third outcome is that traffic is blocked in both directions while men with cutting equipment try to separate the parts of the wreckage belonging to the ex-overtaker from those belonging to his ex-vehicle.

~~~~~

Gendarmes are blind to these transgressions.

Gendarmes who can spot an unfastened seat belt at 100 metres or, with electronic help, a car going 3kph over the speed limit seem to be oblivious to cars tailgating at 120kph or playing Russian roulette on blind bends. Policing of these unfortunate tendencies has been made easier by the introduction of traffic helicopters, but these are used mainly above motorways, where there aren't any blind bends or (at least in theory) oncoming traffic.

~~~~~

Signposting is capricious, to say the least.

Forget about road numbers, for a start. The French don't go in for numbering roads and highways the way the British and Americans do. This isn't to say that roads aren't numbered, it's rather that you aren't always told what the numbers are, or at what point they change to other numbers.

As for road signs, some give only the major destinations ahead, others mention only the next big city you will encounter, and still others – the majority – feature every place you will pass through that has a name. Some indicate the distances involved, some don't.

Most important towns and cities are signposted, one way or another, until you're almost there. Then the signs have a way of disappearing, or giving way to signs for places beyond the next town or city. The best way to avoid getting lost on short journeys is to memorise or note down the names of places both before and after your destination, so that at least you will know when you're headed in the right direction. For longer trips, the Automobile Association has an excellent route-planning service, free on the internet, which gives precise and easy-to-follow directions to and from anywhere in France.

Another problem with French signs is that, unless you're used to driving in France, it isn't immediately clear where the signs are pointed. In this respect they're brilliantly emblematic of French logic: instead of pointing in the direction you wish to go, they point to the road you will have to take to get there. Thus, signs for straight ahead will not point upwards, as in most countries, but will be angled to the left or right to indicate the road going straight ahead.

Lastly, if you find yourself lost in a town, follow the signs to *centre ville*. There, if your intended destination isn't marked, follow the signs saying *toutes directions*. If that fails, try the *autres directions*. Or, of course, you can always stop and ask someone: "*Pour aller . . . ?*"

~~~~~

Expect to keep coming across Messrs Jaurès and Gambetta.

Sooner or later you will begin to wonder why every town you visit has a street named after Jean Jaurès or Léon Gambetta. Who were these worthies in whose honour so much of France was paved? Well, Jean Jaurès was a founder of the French Socialist Party and the newspaper *L'Humanité*; he was assassinated shortly before the First World War. Léon Gambetta was instrumental in proclaiming the Third Republic in 1870, and was briefly Prime Minister a decade later. Now you know.

~~~~~

The autoroutes are a blessing.

Although they're expensive compared to toll roads in other countries, French motorways are still good value if you're on a tight schedule. The toll charges average out at around €0.07 per kilometre, so a trip from Calais to Montpellier will cost you around €65, which isn't bad considering the relatively low fuel prices. Moreover, thanks to a speed limit of 130kph and the lowest traffic density of any motorways in Europe, one can cover great distances quickly and comfortably – and safely, for *autoroutes* are also the safest roads in France.

~~~~~

But Big Brother is watching you.

Until recently, speed limits were enforced retrospectively. When you passed through the *péage*, or toll booth, on leaving an *autoroute*, the computer that calculated the amount due would also compute your average speed since joining the road. The toll booth operator then had discretionary powers to fine you if your average speed was above the limit. But thanks to the abundance of *aires de repos* (rest areas) with restaurants and shops and picnic areas along the way, one could drive at blazing speeds between pit stops and still maintain a legal average. Speed cameras have now been introduced to discourage this.

~~~~~

There's no highway code.

That's to say that there's no single official version but several different versions of the French highway code, published by different publishers, so even the French are somewhat hazy about the laws.

~~~~~

Some laws are stricter than others.

The first law, I suppose it goes without saying, is to have your papers with you (which need not include an international driving licence, provided you have a valid licence of some kind with you). The top permitted speed is 130kph, which applies on most motorways in good weather, but which some drivers still regard as no more than a suggestion. It's 110kph on *autoroutes* in rainy weather, although what constitutes 'rainy weather' is a matter of some conjecture. (My own guess is that this rule is like the more bizarre prohibitions in rental agreements: it's there in case they cannot get you on something else.) Also, during daylight hours, there's a minimum speed of 80kph in the outside lane. The speed limit on ordinary dual-carriageways is 110kph, on 'D' roads 90kph, and in built-up areas 70kph if there are green street markings and 50kph if the markings are yellow.

~~~~~

The driver on the right is in the right.

The laws of self-preservation and common sense generally prevail on French roads, with one exception: whenever two or more roads intersect, the driver coming from the right always has priority unless there's a sign to the contrary (as there usually is at roundabouts). So, even if you're on the 'main' road, keep an eye out for traffic approaching from the right, especially if you pass a triangular sign with an X in it or if you come upon a junction where the traffic lights aren't working normally.

~~~~~

The French have long been fascinated by the mechanics of speed.

The first 'self-moving vehicle' was proposed by a Frenchman, Jacques Ozanam, in 1696. When another Frenchman, a blacksmith named Michaux, added pedals and brakes to the two-wheeled 'velocipede' in 1867, the bicycle was born. Then at the end of the century Edouard Michelin invented the detachable tyre, making possible a really fast bicycle. From there it was but a short step to the Tour de France, the world's greatest bicycle race. The world's first official road speed meeting was organised by the Automobile Club of France and took place, on 18th December 1898, at Achères near Paris, where the impressively named Comte de la Chasseloup-Laubat became the first holder of the world land speed record. In the 20th century, the French pioneered high-speed trains (the *TGV*) and supersonic airliners (the Concorde). So it's perhaps only natural that contemporary representatives of this speed culture should be sitting behind the wheels of French cars.

~~~~~

The Paris roundabouts started out as killing fields.

Back when the area surrounding the capital was heavily forested, landowners created clearings wherever forest paths converged to make it easier to spot game coming out of the trees. These later became roundabouts – where timid drivers are still considered fair game.

~~~~~

When French drivers come to a stop, it's anywhere they like.

In the countryside, those who don't use a tree to stop with tend to park their cars wherever it's likely to cause maximum inconvenience. This can be – and often is – the middle of the road. In the big cities, and especially Paris, a parking space isn't even a prerequisite for parking. As David Hampshire put it in his invaluable *Living and Working in France*, "In Paris, a car is a device used to create parking spaces." It's true. You find cars propped, gouged, squeezed, slanted, wedged into every conceivable space. It makes you wonder if there is such a thing as a reverse-domino effect: could a dozen or so strategically parked cars immobilise all others simply by staying put? Now there's a thought.

15.

SOME SURPRISING THINGS ABOUT

FRENCH
PUBLIC TRANSPORT

The French public transportation system reflects exactly the priorities of its Parisian overseers. Thus it's quick and easy to get around Paris; it's quick and easy to get to or from Paris; it's slow and difficult to get around the rest of France.

~~~~~

You're on your own in the country.

While most cities have excellent municipal bus (and sometimes tram and underground) services, there's no inter-city bus service to speak of. As there are no national bus companies in France operating scheduled routes, you're dependent on private *autocar* or *car* (i.e. bus) services in rural areas or between cities. In some cases these are long-distance tour buses.

In all cases the service is unreliable, and may cease altogether during school holidays.

~~~~~

No point in Paris is more than 500 metres from a Métro station.

Blanketing Paris with 370 stations on 14 lines, the *Métro* is a delight to use.

~~~~~

There are occasional interruptions to the service.

In London, underground announcements usually concern a breakdown or equipment failure; in Paris, the unwelcome news over the loudspeakers is more likely to begin: '*Suite à un mouvement sociale* . . .' – 'As a result of strike action . . .'

The Métro and the RER aren't the same.

The *Réseau Express Régional* (RER) is the modern underground express system that reaches much further out into the Paris suburbs. It also has fewer central Paris stops, and the stations it does share with the *Métro* don't always have the same names. For instance, the Opéra station on the *Métro* is the Auber station on the RER.

~~~~~

France has the largest rail network in Europe.

With 5,000 passenger stations and over 31,000km of track, it carries more than 800 million passengers annually.

~~~~~

The TGV is never early.

The pride of the network, the *TGV*, travels at up to 300kph and serves all major European cities. If a *TGV* is over 30 minutes late the driver is fined, unless he has a very good excuse, and you will be refunded 30 per cent of your ticket price even if he has. (If he's early, he will wait outside the station until the exact moment when the train is due to arrive.) Reservations are required for all journeys, and the difference in cost between first-class and second-class fares is quite small.

~~~~~

You must punch your own ticket.

When travelling by train you must validate your own ticket by inserting it in an orange (soon to be blue) 'composting' machine at the entrance to the platform. This can be done well in advance if you like, but the stamped ticket is only valid for 24 hours. If your ticket hasn't been stamped before you board the train, you could face a stiff fine.

~~~~~

When using French trains, take your own picnic.

Although the *TGV* and other fast trains have a bar-buffet service, the food is uniformly poor and expensive (and sometimes non-existent). It's much wiser to take your own food and drink.

~~~~~

Don't try hailing a taxi in Paris – or anywhere else.

Although there are 15,000 taxis in Paris, they shrink to the point of invisibility when it rains. But rain or shine, your best bet is to find a taxi rank (or, failing that, a large hotel). The same goes for all other major cities. Outside the cities, you will be lucky to find somebody who has ever seen a taxi.

~~~~~

If you're travelling en bloc by taxi, make arrangements beforehand.

Very few taxis will accept as many as four passengers without a prior request by telephone.

16.

SOME SURPRISING THINGS ABOUT
FRENCH HOUSING

The French didn't really know what a housing boom was until the boom in British house prices spiralled out of sight in the '90s, sending swarms of prospective house-buyers across the Channel in search of bargains. And they found them.

One reason is that the French have never regarded houses as a particularly attractive investment. Almost half would prefer to live in apartments anyway. And those who do own houses either tend to keep them as holiday homes or income-producing *gîtes*. So the demand hasn't been there to force up prices. Even the normal inflationary pressures have been siphoned off by the relentless migration of young people to the cities, leaving behind some delectable properties for the invading Anglo-Saxons to scoop up.

As a result, the dormant French housing market has suddenly awakened, rising by almost 15 per cent over the past year, and by even more in the fashionable areas of the south and south-west. Add to this the seemingly inexhaustible barrage of British TV programmes devoted to the delights of living abroad, and there can be little doubt that house prices will continue their dramatic rise for the foreseeable future.

~~~~~

The French are less than delighted at the windfall from property values.

It's true that the British and other foreigners bring money into areas that could do with an infusion of cash, and they usually prefer to buy the sort of properties that don't appeal to the French: old houses and barns in need of renovation. On the other hand, by driving up property values in general they often push house prices beyond what the locals can afford. This can not only lead to resentment of the new arrivals, even extending to instances of vandalism, but can also precipitate open warfare between locals. A recent conference held by the General Council of a *département* in the Midi newly serviced by Ryanair descended into a violent shouting match between those who had profited from the sudden influx of Britons and those who hadn't.

~~~~~

When house hunting, the last place to go is an estate agent's.

Two of the best sources of advance or inside information about properties coming up for sale are the local *notaire*, who will probably handle any eventual transaction for you anyway, and a local postman, who is often the first to know if anyone on his rounds is thinking of selling.

~~~~~

You cannot simply pull out of a purchase.

Once you've found something you like and have agreed a purchase price, you will be expected to sign a *compromis de vente* (provisional sales agreement) and to pay a 10 per cent deposit. If you change your mind later, you forfeit the deposit and may even be obliged to go through with the purchase.

~~~~~

It isn't always warm in the south.

Just because the weather was balmy when you were here doesn't mean that it cannot be glacial in winter. I've often been to stay with friends who own a chateau in the Midi with a lovely swimming pool, yet my abiding memory is not of summer afternoons by the pool but of winter nights looking at ice in the loo.

You don't always get what you see.

If you're buying a house that has been recently occupied, get an itemised list of what the current owners are taking with them and what they're leaving behind. This sounds like acquisitive nit-picking, but it's only a sensible precaution, as the French are inclined to take everything that can be removed without collapsing the house. An English friend recently bought a charming house near Limoges, only to have her first visit as the new owner ruined by the discovery that the previous owners had stripped it of all electrical fixtures and fittings, built-in cupboards, curtain rods, towel rails, radiators, television aerial, mantelpiece – everything, down to and including the kitchen sink.

~~~~~

Shutters are for shutting.

This is only partly for the obvious reason: that shutters act as primitive thermostats, keeping out extremes of cold in winter and heat in summer. Another part-answer is the French penchant for privacy. But the real reason is that it's a habit, formed centuries ago – at a time when rates of taxation were based on 'apparent wealth'. The only way of determining the extent of this wealth was by peering inquisitively through people's windows. And the only way of putting a stop to it was to keep the shutters closed. Thus did shutters become the most effective and historically the most popular means of preventing your house from testifying against you.

~~~~~

There's one long-term property investment that's always a gamble.

It's called the *rente viagère* and it works like this. You buy an elderly person's home by paying a small lump sum and then making regular payments to the owner as long as he (or, more usually, she) lives. When she dies, ownership and possession of the house pass to you. In effect, you're betting that the person will die before your profit margin (and patience) wear too thin.

This is normally a safe bet, but it has been known to go spectacularly wrong. The most celebrated instance occurred not long ago and concerned an old woman whose lawyer had bought her house under the terms of a *rente viagère*. By the time she reached 121, the lawyer had long since been dead and his estate was still paying her off.

~~~~~

Buildings are guaranteed.

All builders engaged in the construction or renovation of a house must be covered by insurance that guarantees their work for ten years after completion.

~~~~~

Builders aren't.

The less cheering news is that the two sentences you're likely to hear most often from workmen are "*Ce n'est pas normal*" and "*Je ferai le maximum*". These are usually translated as "This is most unusual" and "I will do my best". What they really mean is "I haven't a clue how this is supposed to work" and "You'll be lucky if I get this done before the middle of next year".

17.

SOME SURPRISING THINGS ABOUT
FRENCH WOMEN

Seductiveness is probably, and rightly, the characteristic most often attributed to French women. There's simply no getting around the fact that French women are seductive in a way that other women aren't. It isn't difficult to spot. Defining it is. To some, it's nothing more than general sexiness brought into sharper focus when needed. To others, it is tactical coquettishness, a ploy to make life more fun, more interesting.

There's certainly an element of both in the Frenchwoman's repertoire of seductiveness, but there's a lot more to it than that. In fact, like so many things in France, it all started with Napoleon, but for whose codifying zeal French women wouldn't have found themselves in a situation requiring the liberating power of seductiveness in the first place.

Of course, not even Napoleon could claim to have been responsible for the inferior place of women in the overall French scheme of things. That's what we have man-made religions for. But where the subjugation of women is concerned, as with so much else, it was Napoleon who codified it in law, classifying women with children, lunatics and criminals as a sub-species of humanity with only limited rights. Women, he declared, are "the property of man as a fruit tree belongs to the gardener."

~~~~~

Since Napoleon, progress has proceeded at the pace of an escargot.

While France was among the first nations to proclaim such noble ideals as equality and brotherhood, the promotion of the underprivileged at the expense of the inheritors of privilege, the elevation of reason above superstition, it has been among the slowest to recognise and put right the fundamental injustice to women built into French law. Consider these dates from the Frenchwoman's calendar:

1923 Married women given the right to open their own mail.

1938 Married women given the right to obtain a passport without their husbands' permission.

1944 Women given the right to vote and other basic civil rights.

1968 Married women given the right to join a profession or open a bank account without their husbands' permission.

1974 First woman elected to membership of the Académie Française.

That hardly adds up to a half-century of trail blazing in the interest of *égalité*.

~~~~~

It isn't a lot better today.

Only 10 per cent of parliamentary seats are held by women – the lowest percentage in Europe and only half that of the US. By comparison, women in Scandinavia hold roughly 50 per cent of all political offices. There are still only two women among the 40 'Immortals' who make up the Académie Française.

~~~~~

The Frenchwoman's strategy has been to put femininity at the service of feminism.

Whereas the Frenchman's strategy for getting what he wants has traditionally involved collective action, taking to the streets, storming the barricades, the Frenchwoman's strategy has been infinitely subtler. Finding manipulation more fruitful than confrontation, she prefers to infiltrate the precincts of male dominance and subvert them from within. Using charm and guile, she seduces the male into doing her bidding. Rather than sacrifice her femininity and sex appeal to get results, she uses them. After two centuries of waiting for the rest of the Enlightenment to dawn on the French man, the French woman has decided that it's easier to outwit him than to outwait him.

~~~~~

Nor are dead women held in any higher regard.

There are only two women buried in the Panthéon, and only one *Métro* station is named after a woman.

18.

SOME SURPRISING THINGS ABOUT
FRENCH RELIGION

F rance is a Catholic country – true or false? Actually, it's both true and false, thereby summarising the paradox that lies at the heart of French beliefs. More accurately, perhaps, one should say that it's a vigorously secular nation inside an ancient Christian country.

~~~~~

Confession may no longer attract many parishioners, but confessionals do.

They're frequently sold as birdcages at *brocantes* and antiques fairs.

~~~~~

It was the monarchy that inadvertently marginalised the Church.

By insisting on the divine right of kings, the French monarchy ensured that anti-royalist sentiment would become entangled with anti-ecclesiastical feelings, and vice versa, so that popular resentment against one inevitably weakened the other. Thus when France had her revolution, to take one particularly violent example, the beheading of Marie Antoinette was accompanied by the smashing of statues of the Madonna.

~~~~~

Even before the Revolution, the French had a problematical relationship with Rome.

With the conversion of Clovis, king of the Franks, in 496, France became 'the eldest daughter of the Church of Rome', but she would often prove to be a most troublesome daughter. The only Crusade against Christians in a Christian country was launched against the French (by Pope Innocent III in 1209). Indeed, the Inquisition was originally established to root out heresy among the French. And the only direct challenge to the authority of Rome came, in the 14th century, from the French, through the Avignon popes.

~~~~~

Since 1905 there has been rigid separation of Church and State.

The last third of the 19th century was marked by a power struggle between the civil and religious authorities. Finally, in 1902, the state closed 3,000 religious establishments and in 1905 enacted a law specifically aimed at protecting schools from religious interference. The recent ban on the wearing of headscarves, skull caps or large crucifixes was merely a reinforcement of this principle of keeping religion – any religion – out of schools.

~~~~~

Religious wedding ceremonies aren't recognised in France.

For a French marriage to be legally recognised, it must take place before the civil authorities. This may be – and usually is – followed by a ceremony in church, but the religious 'marriage' has no legal status.

~~~~~

France has the largest Muslim and Jewish populations in Europe.

There are an estimated 5 million Muslims in France, as well as 600,000 Jews (and a similar number of Buddhists). Of all the many religions represented in the country, only the Muslims have demanded exemption from the laws of the state.

Anti-Semitism is still alive and kicking.

Although one seldom comes across the sort of crude anti-Semitism that fuelled the Dreyfus affair at the turn of the 20th century or surfaced in the abusive campaigns against prime ministers Léon Blum in the 1930s and Pierre Mendès-France in the 1950s, the type of deep-seated bigotry that contributed to the collaborationist zeal of Vichy, which sent 76,000 French Jews to their deaths in Nazi extermination camps, can still be found smouldering among radical Muslims and the angry halfwits who follow Jean-Marie Le Pen.

~~~~~

The French still exit through the church door.

Although they may be 'christened' by state registrars, and married by civil officials, and during their lifetimes only 8 per cent of them attend Mass regularly, most of the departed French nonetheless have the Last Rites of the Church and then a religious funeral followed by burial in consecrated ground. It's a very French solution to a potentially awkward situation in the hereafter.

19.

SOME SURPRISING THINGS ABOUT

FRENCH
ATTITUDES TO SEX

To understand French attitudes to sex, it is first necessary to understand that considerations of love and marriage are completely irrelevant where sex is concerned. Love belongs to the province of Friendship, and marriage comes under Family. Sex belongs to Romance. It is this link, this element of style in the gratification of physical appetites, that gives the French their reputation in the realm of sex. They approach sex as they approach food: they know that without its ceremonial aspect, it loses much of its point, and all of its beauty.

~~~~~

There's no such thing as a French sex scandal.

Scandals are about bribes, kickbacks, false accounting, influence-peddling; they aren't about sex. French tabloids feature nothing more salacious than public health scares and consumer frauds. Accordingly, there was widespread bafflement over the fuss about President Clinton's fling with Monica Lewinsky. In the words of a Frenchwoman interviewed by an American reporter, "So what? It was only about sex."

Understandably, given this attitude that people's sex lives are none of other people's business, the French took little interest in the fact that President Mitterrand had a mistress and an illegitimate daughter, nor even that he kept both of them in a mansion at taxpayers' expense.

~~~~~

Sex and marriage are coincidental rather than causal.

Nothing better illustrates the discontinuity between the two than the oxymoron *mère célibataire* to describe an unmarried mother. The very fact that the contradictory concepts of motherhood and celibacy can co-exist in the same phrase shows that the real distinction in French thinking is not between married sex and abstention from sex but between procreational and recreational sex.

~~~~~

French girls are among the most demure in Europe.

This will come as a shock to those who assume that a *laisser-aller* (or, as Cole Porter would say, 'anything goes') approach to sex must go hand in hand with promiscuity. In fact, it's only in countries where sex is ringed by taboos, which are then reinforced by peer pressure, that sexual activity represents any kind of liberation. In more sophisticated societies, where the private nature of one's intimate behaviour is part of one's style, modesty and indeed virginity raise fewer eyebrows than indiscriminate sleeping around.

~~~~~

The adjective 'French' is our euphemistic tribute to their openness about sex.

'French love', 'French lessons', 'French tricks', 'French kiss', 'French letter', 'French tickler', 'French sickness': these are all expressions of our quietly envious conviction that if it's naughty, the French must have got there first.

~~~~~

Nudity is a fashion statement, not an erotic advertisement.

As the French aren't prudish about their bodies, they find it difficult to understand how anything so basic to the human condition as nudity could be regarded as obscene. What you don't wear, like what you   wear, is an aesthetic judgment and thus belongs primarily to the world of *couture*. It joins the world of sex at the same point that fashion does, where its main purpose is to stimulate romantic interest.

~~~~~

Prostitution has always been big business in Paris.

In 1474 the Confederation of Harlots in Paris had over 4,000 members. Up until the Revolution, prostitutes attracted customers by reading pornography aloud on street corners. Nowadays there are 20,000 full-time and 60,000 part-time prostitutes working in Paris, most obviously in the vicinity of the railway stations and the Bois de Boulogne.

~~~~~

Pictorial pornography began in Paris.

It wasn't long after Louis Daguerre invented his photographic process in 1839 that Paris was awash with explicitly erotic images for sale. By the 1850s, there were more than 400 photographic studios specialising in bespoke pornography.

~~~~~

The concept of foreplay is alien to French lovemaking.

To the French, lovemaking consists of what we call foreplay. They're one and the same; it's all play and all equally, seamlessly enjoyable. The orgasm is *la petite mort*, the 'little death' that brings the game to an end.

There's an exception to every rule.

Cézanne, arguably the father of modern art, was terrified of women. "I can't have women around," he once confided to Zola. "They disturb my life too much. I don't know what they're for, and I've always been afraid to find out."

~~~~~

The ideal French couple is still together.

Easily the most romantic couple in French history included, almost inevitably, a distinguished philosopher, theologian and logician. After becoming Canon of Notre Dame in Paris in 1115, Pierre Abélard secretly married his pupil and lover Héloïse, who later became a nun and spent over two decades writing him love letters, which still survive. Abélard died in 1142, after relentless persecution by the Church; Héloïse died in 1164. They're buried side by side in a single coffin in the Père Lachaise cemetery in Paris – in a grave which Mark Twain said "has been more revered, more widely known, more written and sung about and wept over . . . than any other in Christendom."

20.

SOME SURPRISING THINGS ABOUT

FRENCH
ATTITUDES TO PETS

The French either indulge their pets shamelessly or neglect them scandalously. There seems to be no middle way. In a country where absurdly pampered dogs munch away at the feet of their owners in chic restaurants, less fortunate dogs – hunting dogs, guard dogs, even ordinary pets – are left locked up or tethered outdoors for weeks at a time in all kinds of weather.

Horses, likewise, tend to be either the beneficiaries of extreme solicitude or the victims of near total disregard for their well-being. I've seen horses that were once promising showjumpers reduced to stumbling, neurotic wrecks from being kept in darkened boxes on sodden hay for unconscionable periods – the equine equivalents of Guantánamo Bay.

~~~~~

France is Europe's largest pet shelter.

France has the highest percentage of homes with pets in Europe. One in three French homes has a dog; one in four has a cat. In a recent survey, 40 per cent of the people questioned named dogs as the most important thing in their lives. Evidence of this can be seen in the fact that they're welcome almost everywhere: in taxis, buses, trains, hotels, restaurants, even most food shops.

~~~~~

The least popular dogs are the food-processing machines that Parisians keep as pets.

There are over half a million dogs in Paris, who deposit on the city's streets an estimated ten tons of excrement per day. As a result, Paris spends more per head on sanitation and street-cleaning than any other city in the world, yet it still remains a dog toilet where an average of 600 people a year break a limb from stepping in the stuff.

The authorities have tried everything they can think of – advertising campaigns, dog loos in the parks, heavy fines – to persuade dog-owners to clean up their act, but all to no avail.

~~~~~

The most popular breed among dog-owners isn't the French poodle.

It's the German Shepherd. No comment.

~~~~~

Don't refer to French pets as 'pets'.

Pet means 'fart' in French. (And *fart* is French for ski wax.) One more reason to keep a dictionary handy.

~~~~~

Always inspect kennels and catteries before using them.

Never entrust a pet to the care of a kennel or cattery without first having a good look at the place. While most are adequate, there are some that on close inspection turn out to have much in common with POW camps.

~~~~~

Autumn and winter walks can be hazardous to your pet's health.

During the hunting season, Frenchmen with shotguns roam the countryside – particularly at weekends, especially after having a few drinks – shooting at everything that moves, including each other. Many pets are killed this way.

21

SOME SURPRISING THINGS ABOUT
FRENCH HUMOUR

If there's one thing that reveals a nation's mentality – a distinguishing characteristic that identifies the mindset of an entire people and sets them apart from others – it must surely be their sense of humour. Who or what makes them laugh? What do they find funny?

Before one can begin to answer these questions with regard to the French, however, you must first ask an even more basic question:

~~~~~

Do the French have a sense of humour?

Not as the British understand the term, certainly. Indeed, the noun *humour* wasn't even approved by the Académie Française until 1932 (although they had somehow let *humoristique* slip through back in 1878). So the French have officially had a sense of humour for three-quarters of a century, although unofficially the suspicion lingers that the Immortals were being uncharacteristically open-minded when they allowed the French to classify what they find funny as 'humour'.

~~~~~

There's one type of joke that the French are congenitally incapable of understanding.

Throughout the English-speaking world – in some places admittedly more so than in others – the absurd is a key element in humour. But to the French (or perhaps one should say Cartesian) mind, anything that derails logic wrecks the joke. As an example of the sort of joke that the French would find incomprehensible, *The Economist* in 2003 chose the one about the governor of the Bank of England who begins his speech to an assembly of bankers by saying, "There are three types of economist – those who can count and those who can't." To our ears, this is a funny joke on several levels; to French ears, it's gibberish.

~~~~~

The French can split their sides at a pun . . .

Subtle wordplay of all kinds, as found in the typical *jeu de mots*, forms the backbone of French wit. For example, there's a hairdressing salon in a town near where I live called '*Quoi faire?*', which is not only a pun on *coiffeur*, or hairdresser, but also the first question the hairdresser asks a client: "What would you like me to do?"

~~~~~

. . . and fall about over falling about.

Given the emphasis on the witty and cerebral in Gallic humour, one is continually amazed to find the French being reduced to helpless laughter by the wordless comedy of Marcel Marceau and the mindless pratfalls of Jerry Lewis. That the French, of all people, should find these two funny – arguably the two unfunniest men on the planet – is a mystery that still awaits plausible explication.

~~~~~

The French have great difficulty in laughing at themselves.

So do most people. But the French have a special terror of appearing ridiculous or laughable. Whereas both British humour and American (particularly Jewish-American) humour specialise in degrees of self-deprecation, the French are distinctly uncomfortable with laughter directed at themselves. Which is perhaps why there's a certain retaliatory edge to their jokes about *les Anglo-Saxons*, while the butts of the simple putdowns are mainly the Belgians and the Swiss. (The really nasty jokes, of course, are reserved for the Parisians.)

Some would maintain that this notion that the French can't laugh at themselves is contradicted by the phenomenon of *Clochemerle*, the book originally published in 1934 which amusingly chronicled how a French village fell out over the construction of a public toilet. While the book was later made into a hit TV series in Britain, in France *Clochemerle* entered the language as a metaphor for the classic dysfunctional village. Nonetheless, to cite this as evidence that the French can easily laugh at themselves is to ignore the fact that dim, feuding villagers are stock characters in the comedy of virtually every nation. In this respect at least, the French are no different from everybody else.

22.

SOME SURPRISING THINGS ABOUT

FRENCH NUMBERS

While the French may mourn the passing of their language as one of the world's preferred means of communication, they can nonetheless take pride in the fact that most of the world now weighs and measures things the French way. The metric system is a French invention. The result, according to Alan Coren, is that the French "have a yard which is 3.37 inches longer than anybody else's." First introduced in 1795, it was given legal status in 1799.

~~~~~

Destinations on road signs are nearer than you think.

A kilometre is less than two-thirds of a mile (0.62 to be precise). Therefore, when you see a sign that says 'PARIS 320' you are in fact only 198 miles from Paris. By the same token, if you see that the speed limit is 90, that isn't a cue to step on it; 90kph is under 56mph. And the top permissible speed on motorways – 130kph – is in fact just a fraction over 80mph. And if you're trying to make sense of the price of fuel, remember that British and American cubic measurements are different. The imperial gallon is 4.54 litres, whereas the American gallon contains only 3.78 litres.

~~~~~

On cars, numbers speak louder than words.

As the last two digits of your French car registration (or licence plate) number correspond to the number of your *département* – e.g. 24 is the Dordogne, 42 is the Loire, and so on – people can tell at a glance where you're from. More to the point, they can tell where you **aren't** from. So, while your car's number may signal that you're more or less a neighbour to others in your *département*, it marks you out as a stranger in the other 95 *départements*. And, as we know, the French don't like strangers. In fact, there are reports disturbingly often of cars, inoffensively parked, being vandalised for no other reason than that their number plates gave them away as 'foreign'.

It probably goes without saying that the number attracting the most consistently hostile attention is 75, which is spelt P-a-r-i-s.

~~~~~

On the street, the next number may not be on the next house.

The house numbered 18 *bis* or 72 *bis* will always be the next house after 18 or 72, not an annex or the flat upstairs. (On road signs, *itinéraire bis* means 'alternative route'.)

~~~~~

A pound isn't a pound (or a book).

A kilogram being 2.2 pounds, half a kilo is of course 1.1 pounds and yet the French, instinctively reverting to pre-Revolutionary measurement systems, call it a 'pound' – *une livre* (not to be confused with *un livre*, which is a book).

~~~~~

The euro hasn't yet caught on throughout France.

Although the franc is neither legal nor in circulation any more, having been replaced years ago by the euro, there are people who still insist on giving prices in francs, and quite often bills payable in euros will give the equivalent amount due in francs, even though they cannot be paid in anything but euros. One might be tempted to put this down to a rather touching need to cling on to the past if it were not for the fact that in more remote parts of the country, where the end of the road is the end of the world, prices are still calculated in **old** francs, which were discontinued in 1958. And, in the thickly cobwebbed corners of the Hexagon, many of the old slang terms for francs survive, such as *balles* (bullets) for francs and *une brique* for a million (old francs, of course).

~~~~~

Commas and decimal points are the wrong way round.

In French figures, a comma is used to separate whole numbers from decimals, and a full stop to separate thousands from hundreds. Thus 6,298.73 is written 6.298,73.

~~~~~

In counting, thumbs count.

In signalling a number by hand, the thumb is always 1. When ordering two of something, for instance, two fingers held up can be understood to mean three (or something else altogether).

~~~~~

The clock doesn't stop at 12.

France, like the rest of continental Europe, goes by the 24-hour clock. It should be a foolproof way of avoiding confusion about the time of day, although American athletes at the Barcelona Olympics missed several preliminary heats by their failure (or inability) to count beyond 12. (In France, they would have been ligitimately befuddled by the maddening French habit of switching back and forth conversationally between the 12- and 24-hour clocks. More maddening still, these sudden conversions are almost always preceded by a look of insufferable sympathy for your chronic inability to get the time right.)

~~~~~

A week has eight days.

A week is referred to by the French as *huit jours*, and a fortnight is called *quinze jours*. This is a way of including the warm embrace of the weekends before and after each.

~~~~~

F1 apartments aren't fast-moving.

In classified advertisements for apartments, the 'F' numbers – F1, F2, F3, etc. – indicate the number of rooms excluding the kitchen, bathrooms and WCs. The really surprising thing, however, is that nobody appears to know what the 'F' stands for.

~~~~~

The French don't have an emergency number; they have four.

In the event of fire and in emergencies requiring an ambulance and paramedics, you must dial 18. If you need 'only' an ambulance, the number is 15. If the police are urgently needed, it's 17. But if you're calling from a mobile phone, the number for all emergencies is 112. Think you can remember all that – in an emergency?

23.

SOME SURPRISING THINGS ABOUT
FRENCH
COUNTRY LIFE

Most country life in France doesn't take place in the countryside; it takes place in the mind, in the imagination, of the French. "Basically, the French are all peasants," Picasso once said, and the French would agree with him. In fact, France is probably the only developed country in the world where the word 'peasant' isn't a pejorative. Every French person, and that includes Parisians, is a *paysan* at heart.

~~~~~

The land has a primeval significance for the French.

There's an old French saying: *"Qui terre a, guerre a"* – "Who has land, has war" – which rather dramatically sums up the ferocity of the French attachment to their land. It's the one thing that can divide families and rupture old loyalties. As the Byzantine emperor Nicephorus I observed many centuries ago, "Have the Frenchman for your friend, not for your neighbour."

~~~~~

It isn't the land in general that attracts French loyalties, but a specific pays.

France is a patchwork of hundreds of *pays*, ancient areas that have nothing to do with the 22 administrative *régions* or 96 *départements* yet still appear on maps and road signs. These *pays* are intimately associated with the local foods and even to specific flavours in the foods from having been grown in specific soils. It isn't merely metaphorical to say that every French person has roots in the soil of his or her own *pays*. Nor is it an exaggeration to say that echoes of one's native *pays* remain in the attitudes as well as the speech of all the French. It was La Rochefoucauld who first pointed out that "the accent of the country where one is born remains in the spirit and the heart as it does in the language."

~~~~~

Even French writers have their own patches.

Francois Mauriac will forever belong to the Bordelais, while Balzac is inextricably linked to the Loire valley, Flaubert to Normandy and Raymond Queneau to Paris, and Frédéric Mistral, Jean Giono and Marcel Pagnol are associated with Provence.

~~~~~

The countryside may be increasingly deserted, but it's productive.

Although in recent years there has been a wholesale exodus from the country to France's five largest cities, leaving behind barely 3 per cent of French workers still engaged in farming, French farmland makes up 22 per cent of the European Union's agricultural surface area, and French agribusiness is by far the EU's largest producer of agricultural products, and the world's second-largest after the US.

~~~~~

French farmers are anything but simple peasants.

This productivity is made possible not by the farmers' proficiency at farming, but by their skill at getting favours from successive French governments and massive subsidies out of the EU. Indeed, so ruthless and single-minded are they at looking after their own interests that *The Times* wrote in 1992: "Britain has football hooligans, Germany has neo-Nazis, and France has farmers."

Paris may be hated but northerners find it irresistible.

While its *grands boulevards* and classical proportions make Paris unarguably one of the world's loveliest cities, it nevertheless sits like a giant spider at the heart of a paved web that draws in and halts traffic from across northern France. Twenty major highways lead into the city, laced together by the *Périphérique*, the notorious ring road that encircles Paris like a misshapen garrotte. Nor is it only road traffic that gets sucked into the metropolis. If anything, the railways are worse. Travelling anywhere by train in northern France without having to change in Paris would tax the ingenuity of even the most dedicated student of timetables. In no other country that I can think of does the capital have such a stifling effect on the movement of so many people in its hinterland.

~~~~~

The wrinkly capital of Europe is the Creuse.

The Creuse *département*, in the Limousin region of central France, has a population with the oldest average age of any area in Europe.

~~~~~

The favourite city of the French is the one that is least like a city.

While it may be the biggest and brightest star in the metropolitan firmament, Paris is by no means the favourite city of the French. In fact, none of the top five can claim that honour. In a recent poll, the French voted Nantes, their sixth-largest and fastest-growing city, 'the best place to live in Europe'. No doubt this is because it comes closest to achieving the perfect marriage of the urban and the rural. A city of 550,000 on the banks of the Erdre where it joins the Loire near the Atlantic coast, it boasts 1,000ha of greenery, 500km of walking and cycling paths, 95 parks and squares, plus a tram network and a fleet of 155 buses that run on natural gas.

~~~~~

The Loire looms large on the weather map as well as road maps.

Just as the north of England is said to begin where the hedgerows end and the stone walls begin, so the Loire marks the dividing line between the northern European climate and the southern.

In addition, France has three climatic zones of its own: the maritime, which extends inland from the Atlantic both north and south of the Loire; the continental, which also shifts up in temperature when it crosses the Loire; and the Mediterranean. Lacking the warm caress of the Gulf Stream to shore up winter temperatures, France can be bitterly cold. Nor does the proximity of the Mediterranean afford any protection. Provence in particular is bone-chilling when the icy Mistral howls in from the north.

~~~~~

La France profonde is profoundly conservative.

The deeper you go into deepest France, the happier the people tend to be about things the way they were. Christopher Booker tells a charming little story which illustrates this perfectly: "In 1988 I was staying with my wife and two small sons in the lovely ancient village of Pegairrolles, tucked into a mountainside at the foot of the *Causses*, those beautiful limestone plateaux north-west of Montpellier, broken by vast gorges. On July 14 the entire community gathered in the small town square for a Bastille Day dinner. We were the only foreigners. As the night wore on under a starlit sky and the prolonged feast came to the time of speeches and toasts, I rose to my feet and solemnly proposed a toast to '*la Révolution*'. After a shocked pause, a number of villagers, only out of politeness, reluctantly stood up to join me. I then proposed a second toast to '*le Conservatisme*'. At once the entire company rose to their feet with a cheer, and enthusiastically drained their glasses."

~~~~~

The French like to build or buy their own retirement homes.

French city-dwellers have more country homes than any other Europeans. These *résidences secondaires* are not only for holidays, but also for retirement. Hence the idiom for 'to retire': '*aller planter les choux*' ('to go and plant cabbages').

~~~~~

The country calendar is different from the city calendar.

In the city, *demain* means 'tomorrow'; in the country, it's a cognate of the Spanish *mañana* – it can mean some time this week, or next, or the week after that, or whenever. It's the same with time spans. Whereas *une quinzaine* is a fortnight in the city, it can stretch into months in the country.

Where workmen and time-based promises are concerned, there's no point in arguing over definitions, or stressing urgency, or threatening to withhold payment. The only thing that works is to drag the workmen's wives into it. This stratagem of genius was devised by Peter Mayle's wife, who suggested inviting the workmen and their wives to a party to celebrate the completion of work as yet undone. The work got done, fast. Ever since reading about this in *A Year in Provence*, I don't bother chasing delinquent workmen. Their wives are much better at it.

Country noses are different from city noses, too.

The concept of BO, or body odour, is virtually unknown in the countryside. The same, alas, cannot be said of the phenomenon itself. Indeed, in its more virulent manifestations, particularly in enclosed spaces, it is enough to bring down a healthy adult at 50 paces.

~~~~~

There are no degrees of 'foreignness' in the countryside.

Whether you're from a different *pays* or a different planet, you're equally foreign in the eyes of rural folk. So there are no built-in advantages or disadvantages if you come from abroad. Of course it helps if you speak French (so long as you don't speak it with a Parisian accent).

~~~~~

Expect power cuts in rural areas.

In certain areas, in fact, they're quite common. Although they tend on the whole to be flickeringly brief, they often last just long enough to stop clocks, ruin settings, and interfere with computers.

~~~~~

Don't expect tree-lined roads.

During the past 30 years over 3 million trees covering a total distance of 20,000km – 90 per cent of all the roadside trees in France – have been cut down in a serial frenzy of state-sponsored vandalism. In one particularly egregious episode, 40km of 200-year-old plane trees near Toulouse were put to the chainsaw to make way for . . . a passing convoy of aeroplane parts.

24.

SOME SURPRISING THINGS ABOUT

FRENCH
RECREATION

To see how seriously the French take their time off, one has only to look at how much of it they award themselves. In addition to five weeks' paid holiday, they get time off for the big public holidays: *Nouvel An*/New Year's Day, *Lundi de Pâques*/Easter Monday, *Fête du Travail*/Labour Day, *Fête de la Libération*/VE Day, *Ascension*/Ascension, *Fête Nationale*/Bastille Day, *l'Assomption*/Assumption, *Toussaint*/All Saints' Day, *Armistice*/Armistice Day, and *Noël*/Christmas.

Schoolchildren have school holidays lasting 117 days, the longest in the world, and working mothers receive 16 weeks' maternity leave at full pay in addition to their five weeks of paid holiday.

~~~~~

Frenchmen like to kill time by killing animals.

Since the right to hunt was made universal in 1871 under the Third Republic, *la chasse* (hunting) has grown in popularity. There are now 1.6 million registered hunters in France – more than in all other European countries combined. While their principal quarry is the *sanglier* (wild boar), they also bag large numbers of deer and rabbits. Although hunting within 150 metres of a house is forbidden, they are such bad marksmen, and often so boozed up, that they account for a good many household pets as well every season.

But perhaps the saddest victims of these weekend infantries are the songbirds they blast out of the sky in defiance of European law. This is done on purpose. Hunters even used to hang caged birds in trees to lure other birds into range of their erratic guns. When this practice was banned, in 1998, 150,000 hunters marched through Paris to proclaim their right to shoot migrating birds. And in 2002 the government, bowing to pressure from the hunting lobby, amended its own 1979 directive on wild birds, reducing the surface area of the country in which the birds were protected from 8 per cent to a laughable 2.6 per cent.

~~~~~

Football and rugby are the top spectator sports.

Despite having to draw on a restricted pool of talent, the French national teams in football and rugby – *les bleus* – are regularly among the world's best. This is because boys in the African and Caribbean communities, who supply the best football players, grow up playing football in the streets (and later hone their skills with leading foreign clubs), while in the south-west of France, French rugby's heartland, boys are endowed early with a consuming love for the game.

At their best, when their natural skills and flair combine with tactical cleverness, French football and rugby teams are unbeatable. At their worst, when individualism or indifference undermines the collective effort, they're still watchable. Indeed, part of the appeal of French teams is that you never know which one will turn up on the day: the electrifying one or the disappointing one. (Probably the most extraordinary demonstration of this phenomenon was provided by the French national football team in the 2002 World Cup. Although essentially the same team that won the World Cup four years earlier, it was eliminated in the group phase of the 2002 competition without scoring a single goal.)

~~~~~

The French once had a top cricket team.

The above would suggest that the ideal team sport for the French would be cricket, where one or two dazzling individual performances can make up for any collapse in the rest of the team. As a matter of fact, the French did enter a cricket team in the 1900 Olympics. It took the silver medal.

~~~~~

Individual sports are preferred to team sports.

This could well be a consequence of the fact that state schools have no sports teams or clubs, and 60 per cent of all students have no access to sports grounds or gymnasia. It could also be due in part to the fact that even in team sports the French tend to put more emphasis on individual flair and style than on discipline and teamwork. In any case, tennis and skiing rank behind cycling in popularity among the general public.

~~~~~

Bullfighting is popular in the south of France.

Although bullfighting was originally popular in classical Greece and Rome, and was introduced into Europe by the Moors in the 11th century, we tend to think of it as an exclusively Spanish spectacle. But not only is it very popular in the south of France, it can be argued that the 'best' bullfights in the world take place in the great Roman amphitheatres of Nîmes and Arles. They have the best matadors, who face the fiercest breeds of bull. Moreover, the crowds at French *corridas* are more knowledgeable than those in Spain.

~~~~~

And poker is popular everywhere.

Another game we tend to associate exclusively, and wrongly, with another country – in this case, the US – is poker. It was invented by the French, and was introduced into America by French settlers. You cannot, however, legally play poker for money in France, as all forms of private gambling were outlawed by (who else?) Napoleon. It's thought to be a law more honoured in the breach than in the observance.

~~~~~

Cycling remains the most popular sport.

The passion for cycling is all but universal among the French, reaching its peak every July with the Tour de France, the world's largest sporting event – and most gruelling. It covers some 4,000km and is watched by some 20 million people along the route. Such is the enthusiasm for the event that its popularity has been unaffected by the dominance in recent years of the American Lance Armstrong, although it could be said without too much exaggeration that the second most popular sport in France is trying to catch Armstrong cheating with drugs, especially since the great French cycling hero, Richard Virenque, was himself caught out a few years ago and banned from the Tour for a year.

~~~~~

Some of the best hotels are unlisted.

While some research in advance may be necessary if one has special requirements, part of the fun of travelling in France is discovering little places that are unlisted in the directories or ungraded by the authorities, yet have more to offer than well known (and invariably more expensive) hotels. This is because the official star-rating system is based on quantifiable categories – facilities available, prices charged – and not on the intangibles that make a stopover something out of the ordinary.

To my knowledge, no other country in the world has anything like the range of hotels that France has to offer. This isn't simply because France is the world's most popular tourist destination; it also has a lot to do with the fact that only 12 per cent of the French themselves, although blessed with long stretches of holiday time, go outside France for their holidays. This means that there's accommodation to suit every taste and every budget.

Beyond that, the only useful all-purpose observation I can make is the obvious one: if you have some abiding need that will cause distress if left unfulfilled, go prepared. Take with you whatever you might suddenly need. In my case it's a small cup, a heating coil and instant espresso. In your case it might be an extra pillow or light bulb. Whatever it is, take it.

And one tip for non-smokers: it's always a good idea to remain uncommitted until you've seen both the smokers' and non-smokers' rooms. Often you will find that all the good non-smoking rooms are already taken, leaving the best of the available rooms for smokers. So be ready to become a theoretical smoker.

~~~~~

The French have two 'awakenings'.

You know the holiday season is approaching when the *pompiers* (firemen) and *facteurs* (postmen) turn up at the door with a 'gift' of next year's calendar, in return for which you may want to make a voluntary 'contribution'. A €20 note should do nicely.

Christmas Eve (or *réveillon* – literally 'awakening') is the focus of Christmas celebrations. During the day you buy and decorate the tree, and in the evening the family gathers for Christmas dinner, traditionally followed by a visit to church for midnight mass

Christmas Day itself is generally given over to recovering from Christmas Eve. Many shops remain open on Christmas Day.

The second *réveillon*, New Year's Eve, also known as St Sylvestre, is the occasion for another feast – usually featuring oysters – plus the usual *pro forma* celebrating at midnight. Twelfth Night, 6th January, is known as *la fête des Rois* (Feast of the Kings) because it commemorates the arrival of the Three Kings bearing gifts for the infant Jesus. In the evening, by tradition, the youngest person present distributes pieces of a special cake, made with puff pastry and almonds, one of which contains a small figurine. Whoever gets it is then crowned king or queen for the day.

Holiday greetings cards are normally sent around this time, not at or before Christmas, with good wishes for the new year. Christmas finally ends on Candlemas (*la Chandeleur*), 2nd February, which is the real French pancake day.

~~~~~

Couch potatoes are cultivated in France, too.

Adults in France spend on average three hours and 20 minutes per day watching television. The figure is unremarkable, unless you've actually watched French television. It is, for the most part, dreadful.

~~~~~

In the summer, the country becomes a festival of festivals.

Wherever you are in June, July or August, somewhere near you there's a town or village *en fête*. France has more festivals than any other country in Europe. And if you like jazz, you won't believe your luck. There are jazz festivals throughout the summer, featuring all the top American jazz musicians. The most famous of these are at Marciac, Vienne, Monségur, Antibes and Juan-les-Pins.

~~~~~

The most enjoyable of all French recreational activities is none of the above.

It's living here – just living here.

THE SAFETY NET

It has often been said that the most valuable information one can have about any subject is simply knowing where to look for the information. On this principle, here is a selection of internet websites where it's possible to find the answers to both common and uncommon questions about France.

General Information

The best all-round website for information about France, with hyperlinks to other sites is:

⌨ www.all-about-france.com

Visitor Information

⌨ www.franceguide.com
⌨ www.francetourism.com
⌨ www.paris-anglo.com
⌨ www.parisinfo.com
⌨ www.tourisme.fr

Travel Information

By Air

⌨ www.airfrance.fr
⌨ www.ba.com
⌨ www.easyjet.co.uk
⌨ www.ryanair.com

By Sea

⌨ www.brittanyferries.co.uk
⌨ www.hoverspeed.co.uk
⌨ www.norfolkline.com

- www.poferries.com
- www.seafrance.co.uk

By Train

- www.raileurope.co.uk
- www.sncf.fr

By Car

- www.eurotunnel.com

By Coach

- www.eurolines.com

Hotel & Restaurant Information

Hotels

- www.accorhotels.com
- www.france-hotel-guide.com
- www.gitesdefrance.com
- www.hotelformule1.com
- www.logis-de-france.fr
- www.loisirsdefrance.com
- www.relaischateaux.fr
- www.vvf-vacances.fr

Restaurants

- www.gaultmillau.fr
- www.grandes-tables.com
- www.viamichelin.com

Cultural Information

- www.americanlibraryinparis.org
- www.bnf.fr (Bibliothèque nationale)
- www.culture.fr
- www.infoconcert.com
- www.louvre.fr
- www.museums-of-paris.com
- www.opera-de-paris.fr
- www.paris.org
- www.pariscope.fr
- www.theatreonline.fr

Language Information

- www.alliancefr.org
- www.bbc.co.uk/education/languages/french
- www.berlitz.com
- www.cesalanguages.com
- www.eurotalk.co.uk
- www.fle.fr/sorbonne
- www.languagesabroad.co.uk
- www.learningfrench.com
- www.parlerparlor.com
- www.therosettastone.co.uk

Educational Information

- www.bip.lon.ac.uk (British Institute)
- www.bls-bordeaux.com
- www.britishcouncil.fr
- www.cordonbleu.net
- www.ecis.org/bsp (British School of Paris)
- www.education.fr
- www.edufrance.fr

- www.fabert.com (parochial schools)
- www.ritz.com
- www.unns.net (United Nations Nursery School)

Financial Information

- www.barclays.fr
- www.britline.com
- www.lapostefinance.fr
- www.swift.com
- www.transat.tm.fr

Shopping Information

- www.123achat.com
- www.amazon.com
- www.bhv.fr (DIY and furnishings in Paris)
- www.cdiscount.com (CDs)
- www.cityvox.com (foreign food)
- www.cuisine-vegetarienne.com
- www.darty.fr (household goods)
- www.fnac.com (books, records, audio)
- www.galerieslafayette.com (department stores)
- www.habitat.fr
- www.ikea.fr
- www.mr-bricolage.fr (DIY)
- www.msn.fr/shopping
- www.shop.com (foreign food)

Motoring Information

- www.IGN.com (regional road maps)
- www.theaa.com (Automobile Association)
- www.trafic.asf.fr (current road works)
- www.viamichelin.com

Car Hire

- www.alamo.com
- www.avis.com
- www.budget.com
- www.hertz.com

Breakdown Service

- www.europ-assistance.com

Medical Information

- www.american-hospital.org
- www.annuaire-assoc-sante.com (health associations)
- www.wice-paris.org (expatriate advisory service)

Private Health Insurance

- www.bcbs.com (Blue Cross & Blue Shield)
- www.bupa-intl.com
- www.expacare.net
- www.norwichunion.co.uk
- www.ppphealthcare.co.uk

Information for Women

- www.aaweparis.org (American Wives of Europeans)
- www.infofemmes.com
- www.planning-familial.org
- www.sosbebe.org (pregnancy counselling)

Information for the Disabled

- www.apf.asso.fr
- www.franceguide.com
- www.vita-vie.com

Information about Pets

- www.defra.gov.uk (pet passports)
- www.royalcanin.fr (kennels)
- www.spa.asso.fr (French 'RSPCA')

TV & Radio Information

French TV

- www.arte-tv.com
- www.canalplus.fr
- www.france5.fr
- www.tf1.fr
- www.tf2.fr
- www.tf3.fr

Satellite TV

- www.astra.lu
- www.eutelsat.org
- www.freeview.co.uk
- www.sky.com

BBC TV & Radio

- www.bbc.co.uk
- www.bbc.co.uk/radio
- www.bbc.co.uk/worldservice
- www.bbcprime.com
- www.bbcworld.com

French Radio

- www.radiofrance.fr

Property Information

- 🖳 www.anil.org (buying and selling)
- 🖳 www.batiweb.com (renovating)

Estate Agents

- 🖳 www.century21.fr
- 🖳 www.fnaim.fr
- 🖳 www.immostreet.com
- 🖳 www.nexdom.com
- 🖳 www.seloger.com

Information about Recreational Activities

- 🖳 www.ffcc.fr (camping)
- 🖳 www.ffct.org (cycling)
- 🖳 www.ffe.fr (riding)
- 🖳 www.fff.fr (football)
- 🖳 www.ffg.org (golf)
- 🖳 www.ffr.fr (rugby)
- 🖳 www.ffrp.asso.fr (hiking)
- 🖳 www.ffs.fr (skiing)
- 🖳 www.fft.fr (tennis)
- 🖳 www.unpf.fr (fishing)

Information for Expatriates

- 🖳 www.aca.ch (American citizens)
- 🖳 www.amb-usa.fr (American embassy)
- 🖳 www.britishexpat.com
- 🖳 www.expatexchange.com
- 🖳 www.expatica.com
- 🖳 www.expatnetwork.com
- 🖳 www.expatworld.net

LIVING AND WORKING SERIES

Living and Working books are essential reading for anyone planning to spend time abroad, including holiday-home owners, retirees, visitors, business people, migrants, students and even extra-terrestrials! They're packed with important and useful information designed to help you **avoid costly mistakes and save both time and money.** Topics covered include how to:

- Find a job with a good salary & conditions
- Obtain a residence permit
- Avoid and overcome problems
- Find your dream home
- Get the best education for your family
- Make the best use of public transport
- Endure local motoring habits
- Obtain the best health treatment
- Stretch your money further
- Make the most of your leisure time
- Enjoy the local sporting life
- Find the best shopping bargains
- Insure yourself against most eventualities
- Use post office and telephone services
- Do numerous other things not listed above

Living and Working books are the most comprehensive and up-to-date source of practical information available about everyday life abroad. They aren't, however, boring text books, but interesting and entertaining guides written in a highly readable style.

Discover what it's really like to live and work abroad!

Order your copies today by phone, fax, post or email from: Survival Books, PO Box 3780, YEOVIL, BA21 5WX, United Kingdom (☎/🖨 +44 (0)1935-700060, ✉ sales@survivalbooks.net, 🖳 www.survivalbooks.net).

BUYING A HOME SERIES

Buying a Home books, including *Buying, Selling & Letting Property*, are essential reading for anyone planning to purchase property abroad. They're packed with vital information to guide you through the property purchase jungle and help you **avoid the sort of disasters that can turn your dream home into a nightmare!** Topics covered include:

- Avoiding problems
- Choosing the region
- Finding the right home and location
- Estate agents
- Finance, mortgages and taxes
- Home security
- Utilities, heating and air-conditioning
- Moving house and settling in
- Renting and letting
- Permits and visas
- Travelling and communications
- Health and insurance
- Renting a car and driving
- Retirement and starting a business
- And much, much more!

Buying a Home books are the most comprehensive and up-to-date source of information available about buying property abroad. Whether you want a detached house, townhouse or apartment, a holiday or a permanent home, these books will help make your dreams come true.

Save yourself time, trouble and money!

Order your copies today by phone, fax, post or email from: Survival Books, PO Box 3780, YEOVIL, BA21 5WX, United Kingdom (☎/🖷 +44 (0)1935-700060, ✉ sales@survivalbooks.net, 🖳 www.survivalbooks.net).

OTHER SURVIVAL BOOKS

The Alien's Guides: *The Alien's Guides to Britain and France* provide an 'alternative' look at life in these popular countries and will help you to appreciate the peculiarities (in both senses) of the British and French.

The Best Places to Buy a Home in France/Spain: The most comprehensive homebuying guides to France or Spain, containing detailed profiles of the most popular regions, with guides to property prices, amenities and services, employment and planned developments.

Buying, Selling and Letting Property: The most comprehensive and up-to-date source of information available for those intending to buy, sell or let a property in the UK.

Foreigners in France/Spain: Triumphs & Disasters: Real-life experiences of people who have emigrated to France and Spain, recounted in their own words – warts and all!

Lifelines: Essential guides to specific regions of France and Spain, containing everything you need to know about local life. Titles in the series currently include the Costa Blanca, Costa del Sol, Dordogne/Lot, Normandy and Poitou-Charentes; Brittany Lifeline is to be published in summer 2005.

Making a Living: Essential guides to self-employment and starting a business in France and Spain.

Renovating & Maintaining Your French Home: The ultimate guide to renovating and maintaining your dream home in France: what to do and what not to do, how to do it and, most importantly, how much it will cost.

Retiring Abroad: The most comprehensive and up-to-date source of practical information available about retiring to a foreign country, containing profiles of the 20 most popular retirement destinations.

Broaden your horizons with Survival Books!

Order your copies today by phone, fax, post or email from: Survival Books, PO Box 3780, YEOVIL, BA21 5WX, United Kingdom (☎/🖷 +44 (0)1935-700060, ✉ sales@survivalbooks.net, 🖳 www.survivalbooks.net).

Qty.	Title	UK	Europe	World	Total
	The Alien's Guide to Britain	£6.95	£8.95	£12.45	
	The Alien's Guide to France	£6.95	£8.95	£12.45	
	The Best Places to Buy a Home in France	£13.95	£15.95	£19.45	
	The Best Places to Buy a Home in Spain	£13.95	£15.95	£19.45	
	Buying a Home Abroad	£13.95	£15.95	£19.45	
	Buying a Home in Cyprus	£13.95	£15.95	£19.45	
	Buying a Home in Florida	£13.95	£15.95	£19.45	
	Buying a Home in France	£13.95	£15.95	£19.45	
	Buying a Home in Greece	£13.95	£15.95	£19.45	
	Buying a Home in Ireland	£11.95	£13.95	£17.45	
	Buying a Home in Italy	£13.95	£15.95	£19.45	
	Buying a Home in Portugal	£13.95	£15.95	£19.45	
	Buying a Home in South Africa	£13.95	£15.95	£19.45	
	Buying a Home in Spain	£13.95	£15.95	£19.45	
	Buying, Letting & Selling Property	£11.95	£13.95	£17.45	
	Foreigners in France: Triumphs & Disasters	£11.95	£13.95	£17.45	
	Foreigners in Spain: Triumphs & Disasters	£11.95	£13.95	£17.45	
	Costa Blanca Lifeline	£11.95	£13.95	£17.45	
	Costa del Sol Lifeline	£11.95	£13.95	£17.45	
	Dordogne/Lot Lifeline	£11.95	£13.95	£17.45	
	Poitou-Charentes Lifeline	£11.95	£13.95	£17.45	
	Living & Working Abroad	£14.95	£16.95	£20.45	
	Living & Working in America	£14.95	£16.95	£20.45	
	Living & Working in Australia	£14.95	£16.95	£20.45	
	Living & Working in Britain	£14.95	£16.95	£20.45	
	Living & Working in Canada	£16.95	£18.95	£22.45	
	Living & Working in the European Union	£16.95	£18.95	£22.45	
	Living & Working in the Far East	£16.95	£18.95	£22.45	
	Living & Working in France	£14.95	£16.95	£20.45	
	Total carried forward (see over)				

ORDER FORM

Qty.	Title	UK	Europe	World	Total
			Total brought forward		
		Price (incl. p&p)			
		UK	Europe	World	
	Living & Working in Germany	£16.95	£18.95	£22.45	
	L&W in the Gulf States & Saudi Arabia	£16.95	£18.95	£22.45	
	L&W in Holland, Belgium & Luxembourg	£14.95	£16.95	£20.45	
	Living & Working in Ireland	£14.95	£16.95	£20.45	
	Living & Working in Italy	£16.95	£18.95	£22.45	
	Living & Working in London	£13.95	£15.95	£19.45	
	Living & Working in New Zealand	£14.95	£16.95	£20.45	
	Living & Working in Spain	£14.95	£16.95	£20.45	
	Living & Working in Switzerland	£16.95	£18.95	£22.45	
	Making a Living in Spain	£13.95	£15.95	£19.45	
	Normandy Lifeline	£11.95	£13.95	£17.45	
	Renovating & Maintaining Your French Home	£16.95	£18.95	£22.45	
	Retiring Abroad	£14.95	£16.95	£20.45	
				Grand Total	

Order your copies today by phone, fax, post or email from: Survival Books, PO Box 3780, YEOVIL, BA21 5WX, United Kingdom (☎/▤ +44 (0)1935-700060, ✉ sales@ survivalbooks.net, 💻 www.survivalbooks.net). If you aren't entirely satisfied, simply return them to us within 14 days for a full and unconditional refund.

I enclose a cheque for the grand total/Please charge my Amex/Delta/Maestro (Switch)/MasterCard/Visa card as follows. (delete as applicable)

Card No. _ _ _ _   _ _ _ _   _ _ _ _   _ _ _ _   Security Code* _ _ _

Expiry date _____   Issue number (Maestro/Switch only) _____

Signature _____   Tel. No. _____

NAME _____

ADDRESS _____

_____

_____

* The security code is the last three digits on the signature strip.